MADNESS AND SEXUAL POLITICS
IN THE FEMINIST NOVEL

BARBARA HILL RIGNEY

Madness and Sexual Politics in the Feminist Novel

Studies in
Brontë, Woolf,
Lessing,
and Atwood

The University of Wisconsin Press

Published 1978

The University of Wisconsin Press
114 North Murray Street, Madison, Wisconsin 53715

The University of Wisconsin Press, Ltd.
1 Gower Street, London WC1E 6HA, England

Printings 1978, 1980

Printed in the United States of America

ISBN 0-299-07710-1 cloth, 0-299-07714-1 paper
LC 78-53291

To my sister Sandy, who went into the dark,
and to my small women, Jules and Kris,
in the hope they will know her light

CONTENTS

ACKNOWLEDGEMENT

I GRATEFULLY AND AFFECTIONATELY ACKNOWLEDGE the contributions of my parents, George and Juanita Hill, of my husband, Kim Rigney, and of my friends and colleagues Professors Morris Beja, Lowanne Jones, Richard Martin, Ernest Lockridge, Richard Bjornson, Kezia VanMeter Sproat, and Mary Irene Moffitt.

Introduction

THE PSYCHOANALYTIC APPROACH to literary criticism is a well-established subject of inquiry. However, a greater part of the feminist movement has considered modern psychology to be both a product and a defense of the status quo—a patriarchal society. *Madness and Sexual Politics in the Feminist Novel* attempts to reconcile feminism and psychology in the area of literary criticism, to find examples in the major works of four representative feminist writers of the relationship between madness and the female condition.

A dissatisfaction with the principles of psychology and psychiatry as exclusively representing male-defined values and standards is almost universal among feminists. "Freud is the father of psychoanalysis. It had no mother," writes Germaine Greer.[1] According to Greer and others, such a parentage results in a double standard for mental health: that which is considered normal and desirable behavior for men is thought to be neurotic or even psychotic for women. The normal woman, according to Phyllis Chesler in *Women and Madness*, is often defined by psychologists as the housewife, content with passivity and limited authenticity.[2] In a society which values competition, material success, aggressiveness—characteristics considered to be essentially masculine and therefore discouraged in women—

3

femininity becomes a negative quality. Thus, Chesler asserts, psychotherapy reflects a society which devalues women and socializes them to devalue themselves.

A majority of feminist writers, psychologists, and philosophers have held Freud culpable for psychology's treatment of women. A series of authorities, beginning with psychiatrist Karen Horney in the 1920s, have concerned themselves with a refutation of such Freudian theories as the female castration complex and the vaginal orgasm.[3] Horney's followers in this area include such psychiatrists as Clara Thompson, Ruth Moulton, and Alexandra Symonds, some of whose works in this area are included in Jean Baker Miller's anthology *Psychoanalysis and Women*.[4] The more political and philosophical aspects of Freudian psychoanalysis arc analyzed by Simone de Beauvoir in *The Second Sex*, Shulamith Firestone in *The Dialectics of Sex*, Betty Friedan in *The Feminine Mystique*, and Kate Millet in *Sexual Politics*, to name a few, all of whom have devoted major portions of their works to castigations of Freud. Millett, for example, sees Freud as "beyond question the strongest individual counterrevolutionary force in the ideology of sexual politics" during his period.[5]

The techniques employed by post-Freudian psychoanalysts in the therapeutic process are also considered by many feminists to be damaging to women's self-images. Chesler, in an article entitled "Patient and Patriarch: Women in the Psychotherapeutic Relationship," maintains that analytic techniques are often power oriented, paternalistic, and coercive:

> Freud believed that the psychoanalyst-patient relationship must be that of "a superior and a subordinate." The psychotherapist has been seen—by his critics as well as his patients—as a surrogate parent (father or mother), savior, lover, expert, and teacher—all roles that foster "submission, dependency, and infantilism" in the pa-

tient: roles that imply the therapist's omniscient and be-
nevolent superiority and the patient's inferiority.[6]

Chesler further states that psychotherapy reinforces
the rigidity of sex roles as seen in social institutions like
marriage. Both psychotherapy and marriage, she writes,

> are based on a woman's helplessness and dependency on
> a stronger male authority figure; both may, in fact, be
> viewed as reenactments of a little girl's relation to her
> father in a patriarchal society; both control and oppress
> women similarly—yet, at the same time, are the two
> safest havens for women in a society that offers them no
> others.[7]

Psychologist Naomi Weisstein regards such traditional
psychotherapeutic methods and theories as strangling
and deflecting any positive achievements toward understanding psychosis in women: "It then goes without saying that present psychology is less than worthless in contributing to a vision which could truly liberate—men as
well as women."[8]

Jean Baker Miller, also in disagreement with post-
Freudian techniques, suggests alternatives:

> The belief that women could or should accept and adjust
> to the stereotyped role has been a cause, not the cure, of
> their problems. From this new perspective, they then
> suggest many exciting reorientations for therapy. One
> permits all so-called symptoms to be seen in a new
> light—no longer merely as defenses, maneuvers, or
> other such tactics, but as struggles to preserve or express
> some deeply needed aspects of personal integrity in a
> milieu that will not allow for their direct expression. The
> task of a therapist then becomes the cooperative search
> for an understanding of those needs and an understand-
> ing of how they have been diverted or distorted.[9]

One of the few feminists who defend Freud is Juliet
Mitchell. In both *Psychoanalysis and Feminism* and *Woman's Estate*, Mitchell blames "post-Freudian empiri-

cism" rather than Freud's original theories, which she
sees as combatting the pernicious social forces they reflected. Freud, she maintains, "partook of the social
mores and ideology of his time whilst he developed a
science that could overthrow them."[10] Mitchell also
states that Freudian theory "is not a recommendation *for*
a patriarchal society, but an analysis *of* one."[11]

It seems very difficult, however, to separate Freud's
intentions from his practices. The feminist feud with
Freud is more basic than a disagreement over the issues
of female sexuality or therapeutic technique. The real
quarrel is one of fundamental ideology: Freud's deterministic philosophy, what Weisstein terms "the fun-
damentalist myth of sex organ causality,"[12] is perceived
by others than Mitchell as invalidating social and cultural explanations for psychosis. Most feminists see
madness, first, as a political event. Female insanity, they
argue, can in a majority of cases be explained by the
oppression of women in a power-structured, male-
supremacist society. According to Kate Millett,

> when in any group of persons, the ego is subjected to
> such invidious versions of itself through social beliefs,
> ideology, and tradition, the effect is bound to be perni-
> cious. This coupled with the persistent though fre-
> quently subtle denigrations women encounter daily
> through personal contacts, the impressions gathered
> from the images and media about them, and the dis-
> crimination in matters of behavior, employment, and
> education which they endure, should make it no very
> special cause for surprise that women develop group
> characteristics common to those who suffer minority
> status and a marginal existence.[13]

Chesler's statement is equally strong: she describes
madness in women as "an intense experience of female
biological, sexual, and cultural castration, and a doomed
search for potency."[14]

Thus, Freud's deterministic theories are denied, and

the negative experience of women is seen as a cultural phenomenon rather than as an anatomical inevitability. Ideally, psychoanalytic theories should not work to force women into roles society has dictated, but rather should define women as individuals capable of both freedom and responsibility.

Most of the novels under consideration in the following chapters do accomplish such an affirmation. Charlotte Brontë in *Jane Eyre*, Virginia Woolf in *Mrs. Dalloway*, Doris Lessing in *The Four-Gated City*, and Margaret Atwood in *Surfacing* all depict insanity in relation to sexual politics and state that madness, to a greater or lesser degree, is connected to the female social condition. Each novel presents a criticism of a patriarchal political and social system, a universe dominated by masculine energy, which, in itself, manifests a kind of collusive madness in the form of war or sexual oppression and is thereby seen as threatening to feminine psychological survival. Most of these novels depict a female protagonist who, in spite of such oppression, achieves a superior sanity and at least a relative liberty in the assertion of a self.

The language and the ideology of orthodox psychology are useless for such a feminist analysis. However, one of the few counterideologies which does apply is that of R. D. Laing. To be sure, Laing cannot be seen essentially as a feminist, having written relatively little about women, and then depicting them primarily as destructive mothers. He does not, as Miller points out, concern himself with the inappropriateness of psychoanalysis as applied specifically to women.[15] Too, he has been accused by more traditional practitioners, perhaps unjustifiably, of romanticizing insanity and thereby recommending withdrawal and paralysis, techniques antipathetic to feminists.

Yet, Laing's revolutionary approach to both philoso-

phy and psychoanalysis can provide at least a terminol-
ogy, a framework, convenient for feminist protest. Even
Mitchell, who sees Laing's theories as extremely dubi-
ous, is forced to admit his contribution to political ideology and language.[16] Lessing's acknowledged debt to
Laing will become obvious in the chapter on *The Four-
Gated City*. Elizabeth Janeway repeatedly quotes from
Laing in her analysis of the traditional family in *Man's
World, Woman's Place*.[17] In the absence of any other
available and widely recognized authority, then, Laing
may serve to provide a base from which to begin a
feminist psychoanalytic approach to literature.

Laing's relevant theories, which Mitchell terms examples of "radical humanism,"[18] include the conviction
that psychosis, whether in women or in men, is an
understandable or even a "sane" response to life in a
destructive society. Schizophrenia, Laing says, "is a special strategy that a person invents in order to live in an
unlivable situation."[19] Lessing's Martha Quest Hesse
and Woolf's Septimus Warren Smith, in particular, provide literary examples in support of the validity of such
a contention. Schizophrenia is, however, for Laing and
for the writers to be discussed, only a kind of temporary
answer to social and political oppression. Madness is but
a stage in the evolution of a conscious, truly sane person.
As Jungian myth criticism has revealed, all heroes must
pass through a phase of withdrawal and deep introspec-
tion before they can return as lawgivers. What Laing
refers to throughout his works as "superior sanity" is
achieved only through the experience of recognizing
the general illness of society and its subjective implica-
tions. One can never be truly *well*, it might be argued,
unless illness is identified and rejected, never whole unless divisions are seen and mended. The return, then,
and not the insanity itself, is what Laing and the feminist
novelists to be discussed have chosen to celebrate.

Also useful in a feminist analysis are Laing's views on Freud. While more flattering to Freud than those held by most feminists, Laing's opinions nevertheless suggest Freud's severe limitations:

> Freud was a hero. He descended to the "Underworld" and met there stark terrors. He carried with him his theory as a Medusa's head which turned these terrors to stone. We who follow Freud have the benefit of the knowledge he brought back with him and conveyed to us. He survived. We must see if we now can survive without using a theory that is in some measure an instrument of defense.[20]

Along with many feminists, Laing sees psychosis at least partly as a revolt against the claustrophobic element of the traditional nuclear family.[21] Much like Virginia Woolf in *Three Guineas*, Laing perceives the family as a microcosm, reflecting the patriarchal and ultimately fascist attitudes prevalent in society as a whole. Throughout his works, Laing attacks the family on political and social grounds, maintaining that parents often destroy their children with possessiveness, with love which is more devastating than hate. Women, as well as children, suffer limitations within the family, Laing states. The very unit which purports to provide women their self-definition, Laing argues, is in reality a seat of authoritarianism, an agent of human and sexual repression.

Both women and men are, for Laing, existential entities. Society, however, tends to categorize people into dehumanized and oppositional stereotypes like male and female, sane and insane. Particularly in the later and more radical *Politics of Experience*, Laing echoes many feminists in his plea for the abandonment of role prescriptions and the restoration of the *whole* person, the undivided self.

Primarily, it is this sense of the self as divided that is

reflected in the image of the doppelgänger which is so
pervasive and important in the novels to be discussed.
Accepted theories on the function of the double in literature do not seem to apply to the works of these women
writers. Otto Rank in *The Double: A Psychoanalytic Study*
sees the doppelgänger as an insurance against the destruction of the ego and a denial of death.[22] Robert
Rogers in *A Psychoanalytic Study of the Double in Literature*
even less convincingly argues that the mirror image is
"without exception" a manifestation of "narcissim."[23]
For the protagonists analyzed in the following chapters,
however, the doppelgänger seems to represent the recognition of the tragedy of one's own fragmentation and
alienation from the self. According to Laing,

> the others have become instilled in our hearts, and we
> call them ourselves. Each person, not being himself
> either to himself or the other, just as the other is not
> himself to himself or to us, in being another neither
> recognizes himself in the other, nor the other in himself.
> Hence, being at least a double absence, haunted by the
> ghost of his own murdered self, no wonder modern man
> is addicted to other persons, and the more addicted, the
> less satisfied, the more lonely.[24]

As will also be explored in the following analyses, Laing's opposition to traditional psychotherapeutic techniques actually reinforces the feminist arguments. Laing
virtually redefines the analyst-patient relationship:

> Psychotherapy consists in the paring away of all that
> stands between us, the props, masks, roles, lies, defenses,
> anxieties, projections and interjections, in short, all the
> carryovers from the past, transference and counter-
> transference, that we use by habit and collusion, wit-
> tingly or unwittingly, as our currency for relation-
> ships. . . . Of course, such techniques in the hands of a
> man who has not unremitting concern and respect for
> the patient could be disastrous.[25]

The disaster in the works of Brontë, Woolf, Lessing,
and Atwood inevitably lies in the encounter with the

male authority figure, whether lover, husband, father, or psychiatrist, who decides the question of sanity and who then assumes the power to incarcerate and to destroy. In Woolf's *Mrs. Dalloway*, the villain is Sir William Bradshaw, the famed psychiatrist who sees all mental illness as a mere "lack of proportion" and who so tragically mishandles Septimus Warren Smith's breakdown. His remedy is to lock people up, thus robbing them of political and existential rights. He is depicted in military images, represented as a kind of warrior, a personification of tyranny. His parallel, only slightly less caricatured, is found in Lessing's *The Four-Gated City* in the character of the ironically named Dr. Lamb, who represents power itself and whose very humanity is in question. In Brontë's *Jane Eyre*, the minister of God is the surrogate psychiatrist. Such hypocrites as the Reverend Brocklehurst and St. John Rivers are equally as insensitive and equally as powerful as the modern physicians depicted by Lessing and Woolf. For Atwood's protagonist of *Surfacing*, male power is totally impersonal, embodied in a group of oppressors she calls "the Americans."

All of the novelists to be discussed present studies of alienated female consciousnesses in opposition to a male society or to individual male authority figures. Each protagonist rejects the father figure and, to varying degrees, embarks on a search for the metaphoric mother. It is significant that both Clarissa Dalloway and Jane Eyre are motherless (as were Woolf and Brontë), and that Martha Quest Hesse has an ineffectual and geographically removed mother. In Atwood's novel, the search for the mother is raised to theological significance. Adrienne Rich, in *Of Woman Born*, sees all women as psychologically crippled, disinherited, and culturally bereft because they have been denied the love of strong figures of their own sex.[26] What each of the protagonists is to discover, however, is that she must find a mother within the self, and so begin the return from psychosis.

Just as Laing perceives the psychotic personality to be a victim of oppression in search of a lost and divided self, so Woolf, Lessing, and Atwood, in particular, see their schizophrenic characters as at least quasi-religious figures, saints or savants, questing for some form of truth. Lessing writes that "it is through madness and its variants" that truth must be sought. Atwood maintains that vision comes only "after the failure of logic." Woolf's mad Septimus becomes, in fact, a Christ figure. Even in *Jane Eyre*, that product of premodern psychology, the mad woman is somehow justified in her hatred and violence: she is a scapegoat rather than a force for evil. Chesler, like Laing, Brontë, Woolf, Lessing, Atwood, and others, endows the schizophrenic with mythic significance:

> Perhaps the angry and weeping women in mental asylums are Amazons returned to earth these many centuries later, each conducting a private and half-remembered search for her motherland—a search we call madness.[27]

A description of numerous such searches—for the mother within the self, for the feminist consciousness of a sense of self-worth—is the subject of the following chapters.

1

"The Frenzied Moment": Sex and Insanity in Jane Eyre

... the lunatic asylum is yellow.

On the first floor there were
women sitting, sewing;
they looked at us sadly, gently,
answered questions.

On the second floor there were
women crouching, thrashing,
tearing off their clothes, screaming;
to us they paid little attention.

On the third floor
I went through a glass-panelled
door into a different kind of room.
It was a hill, with boulders, trees, no houses.

... the air
was about to tell me
all kinds of answers.

Margaret Atwood's "Visit to Toronto with Companions,"
The Journals of Susanna Moodie

> In the deep shade, at the further end of the room, a
> figure ran backwards and forwards. What it was,
> whether beast or human being, one could not, at first
> sight, tell: it grovelled, seemingly on all fours; it snatched
> and growled like some strange wild animal: but it was
> covered with clothing; and a quantity of dark, grizzled
> hair, wild as a mane, hid its head and face.[1]

Charlotte Brontë presents this vision of desexed and
dehumanized insanity in *Jane Eyre* as Bertha Mason,
Rochester's lunatic wife. For ten years, she has been
hidden and confined in a denlike room in the attic of
Thornfield Hall, where she paces and snarls and howls
her tragic and preternatural laugh. Her form is grotesque; her eyes are "red balls," her face "bloated" and
"purple" (370). Madness has caused this metamorphosis
from human into animal, for Bertha was once "the boast
of Spanish Town for her beauty" (389).

Critical interpretations of Bertha's symbolic functions
in *Jane Eyre* are varied and sometimes contradictory. For
traditional critics who see the novel as a form of religious allegory, the mad woman represents the evil in
Rochester's soul from which he must be purified by
purgatorial fires and the ministrations of a devout
woman in the archetypal pattern of sin, suffering, and
redemption.[2] In Freudian terms, Bertha is the evil-

mother figure who prevents Jane's sexual union with the fatherlike Rochester,[3] or she is seen to embody the idlike aspects of Rochester's psyche for which he suffers symbolic castration, blindness being the punishment for sexual crime since Oedipus.[4]

However, Bertha is as much a doppelgänger for Jane as for Rochester: she serves as a distorted mirror image of Jane's own dangerous propensities toward "passion," Brontë's frequent euphemism for sexuality. Bertha embodies the moral example which is the core of Brontë's novel—in a society which itself exhibits a form of psychosis in its oppression of women, the price paid for love and sexual commitment is insanity and death, the loss of self. Female ontological security and psychological survival in a patriarchal Victorian age, Brontë maintains, can be achieved only through a strong feminist consciousness and the affirmation of such interdependent values as chastity and independence.

Many modern psychologists, like R. D. Laing, state that societies themselves can manifest symptoms of psychosis.[5] The Victorian social system, as described by Helene Moglen in her biography of Brontë, reflects a collusive madness in its sexual politics:

> The advent of industrialization and growth of the middle class was accompanied by a more diffuse yet more virulent form of patriarchy than any that had existed before. As men became uniquely responsible for the support of the family, women became "possessions," identified with their "master's" wealth. The status of the male owner derived from the extent of his woman's leisure time and the degree of her emotional and physical dependence upon him. Sexual relationships followed a similar pattern of dominance and submission. Male power was affirmed through an egoistic, aggressive, even violent sexuality. Female sexuality was passive and self-denying. The woman, by wilfully defining herself as "the exploited," as "victim," by seeing herself as she was re-

flected in the male's perception of her, achieved the only
kind of control available to her. Mutuality was extraor-
dinarily difficult, if not impossible, to achieve.[6]

All male characters in *Jane Eyre*, to a greater or lesser
extent depending on their area of influence, are agents
of such a sexually oppressive system. John Reed, the
Reverend Brocklehurst, Rochester, and St. John Rivers,
each of whom is dominant in one of the successive land-
scapes which make up the novel's progress, become a
single symbol of tyranny as they share a common conscious or subconscious desire to render Jane an object, a
Bertha, something less than a human being. Brontë indicates that, were Jane to succumb, to allow her will to
be usurped, she as a sexual and human identity would
cease to exist, just as Bertha Mason has ceased to exist in
both human and sexual terms.

Jane first learns about female powerlessness from her
guardian's son, who is also her cousin, John Reed. Like
most of Brontë's male characters, he is the sole male in a
female community, the members of which accept the
role of self-abnegation deemed rational for women by
society, and accordingly pamper and indulge their male
relative. Jane, for a time, grudgingly assumes the traditional role, as John summons her to receive punishment for an imagined crime:

> Habitually obedient to John, I came up to his chair: he
> spent some three minutes in thrusting out his tongue at
> me as far as he could without damaging the roots: I knew
> he would soon strike, and while dreading the blow, I
> mused on the disgusting and ugly appearance of him
> who would presently deal it. . . . (7)

But Jane is not always "rational" and must retaliate
against such obvious sexual threats: "Wicked and cruel
boy! . . . You are like a murderer—you are like a slave
driver—you are like the roman emperors!" (8) She

bloodies John's nose and is punished, just as Bertha is
later to be punished for analogous acts of revenge, by
confinement. During her imprisonment in "the red
room," significantly a color associated with passion and
a place associated with her uncle's death, Jane experiences a "species of fit" (16), a temporary madness and
loss of consciousness. Jane's own reflection in the great
mirror which dominates the room contributes to her
hysteria.

Moglen describes this episode as one in which "the
principle of irrationality is given concrete form,"[7] and in
which Jane "loses her sense of the boundaries of her
identity."[8] Mrs. Reed tells Jane that she can be liberated
only "on the condition of perfect submission and still-
ness" (16), that is, on the condition of "sane" behavior.

Reverend Brocklehurst is also a lone male oppressor
in a female society, that of Lowood Institution. Jane's
first impression of him is one of tremendous phallic
impact: he was "a black pillar . . . a straight, narrow,
sable-clad shape standing erect on the rug: the grim face
at the top was like a carved mask, placed above the shaft
by way of capital" (33). For the second time, Brontë
associates male sexuality with cruelty and even death.
But unlike John Reed, who only seems to Jane to be a
murderer, Brocklehurst is in fact guilty of indirectly
causing the deaths of numbers of his charges at the
school. He starves their bodies, chastizes their souls with
threats of damnation and hellfire, symbolically desexes
them by cutting their hair, and generally forces them
into submission. Jane escapes the contagious typhoid
which kills many of the debilitated inmates of Lowood
by a self-imposed isolation in the surrounding woods
and valleys.

An analogous withdrawal, and also self-imposed, will
again save Jane from annihilation, this time psychological, in the next phase of the novel. Thornfield Hall is

dominated by the Byronic figure of Rochester, again the only male in residence. In spite of the fact that Rochester is at times gratuitously cruel in his attempts to provoke Jane's jealousy, that he lies on a number of occasions, and that he is attempting the social and religious crime of bigamy, Jane is profoundly tempted to surrender her very self to the magnetism, the sexuality, the male charisma that is Rochester. Brontë has frequently indicated that Jane's longing for love is so intense as to be self-destructive. Jane has confided to her friend Helen Burns:

> . . . if others don't love me, I would rather die than live—
> I cannot bear to be solitary and hated, Helen. Look here;
> to gain some real affection from you, or Miss Temple, or
> any other whom I truly love, I would willingly submit to
> have the bone of my arm broken, or to let a bull toss me,
> or to stand behind a kicking horse, and let it dash its hoof
> at my chest. . . . (80)

Brontë's own letter to the beloved Monsieur Heger bespeaks a painfully similar state of emotion.

> I know that you will be irritated when you read this
> letter. You will say once more that I am hysterical (or
> neurotic)—that I have black thoughts, etc. So be it,
> monsieur, I do not seek to justify myself; I submit to
> every sort of reproach. All I know is, that I cannot, that I
> will not, resign myself to lose wholly the friendship of my
> master. I would rather suffer the greatest physical pain
> than always have my heart lacerated by smarting regrets.
> If my master withdraws his friendship from me entirely
> I shall be altogether without hope; if he gives me a
> little—just a little—I shall be satisfied—happy; I shall
> have a reason for living on, for working.
> Monsieur, the poor have not need of much to sustain
> them—they ask only for the crumbs that fall from the
> rich man's table. But if they are refused the crumbs they
> die of hunger.[9]

Similar images of hunger and starvation recur throughout *Jane Eyre*. Margot Peters, in *Charlotte Brontë:*

Style in the Novel, sees such references as indicative of
Jane's sexual and emotional deprivation.[10] Frequent
references to cold and the desire for warmth serve the
same function. But the fire that is Rochester's passion,
and Jane's as well, becomes volcanic in its intensity: like
Brocklehurst's hellfire, it consumes rather than warms
and is thus perceived by Brontë as ultimately dangerous.

Brontë's frequent use of fire symbolism to represent
passion and sexuality also has psychological significance.
Laing has written in *The Divided Self* that ontologically
insecure people are in constant dread of what he calls
"engulfment," the sense that one may lose one's self in
the identity of another. This fear, writes Laing, is often
expressed in images of both burning and drowning:
"Some psychotics say in the acute phase that they are on
fire, that their bodies are being burned up . . . [they] will
be engulfed by the fire or the water, and either way be
destroyed."[11] It is significant that both Brocklehurst and
St. John Rivers threaten Jane with the fires of damnation, that Helen *Burns* dies an early and sacrificial death,
and that Rochester frequently invites Jane to sit with
him by the fire where both his touch and his glance burn
like coals. Bertha Mason dies as the result of a conflagra-
tion she herself has set. Drowning, too, is a concern of
Jane's: ". . . the waters came into my soul; I sank in deep
mire: I felt no standing; I came into deep waters: the
floods overflowed me" (375). Among Jane's paintings
displayed to Rochester, presumably revelations of her
inner feelings, is one in which "a drowned corpse
glanced through the green water" (153).

It becomes increasingly apparent that what Brontë
fears for Jane is that marriage with Rochester will not be
a union of equals, but rather a loss of self, an engulfment in the identity of another, just as it was for Bertha

Mason. Laing describes a similar fear, which he again attributes to the psychotic personality:

> If one experiences the other as a free agent, one is open to the possibility of experiencing oneself as an *object* of his experience and thereby of feeling one's own subjectivity drained away. One is threatened with the possibility of becoming no more than a thing in the world of the other, without any life for oneself, without any being for oneself. In terms of such anxiety, the very act of experiencing the other as a person is felt as virtually suicidal.[12]

Jane's extreme sense of ontological insecurity, however, need not necessarily be labeled psychotic, as it is surely justified by Rochester's behavior during their courtship period. On hearing from Rochester that she is to become "Jane Rochester," to lose her very name, Jane states that "the feeling, the announcement sent through me, was something stronger than was consistent with joy—something that smote and stunned: it was, I think, almost fear" (325). Rochester becomes progressively more possessive, less cognizant of Jane as a human being with individual tastes and preferences. Despite Jane's remonstrances, he insists on extravagant gifts which serve to emphasize her economic powerlessness: "The more he bought me, the more my cheek burned with a sense of annoyance and degradation" (338).

The image of the slave, notable in Jane's encounter with John Reed, recurs frequently in her relationship with Rochester: "I thought his smile was such as a sultan might, in a blissful and fond moment, bestow on a slave his gold and gems had enriched...." (339) Rochester threatens in response to Jane's withdrawal: "... it is your time now, little tyrant, but it will be mine presently: and once I have fairly seized you, to have and to hold, I'll just—figuratively speaking—attach you to a chain, like this (touching his watch guard)" (341). In the next chapters, Jane will witness Rochester seizing a violent Bertha and binding her with rope.

And, as in Jane's encounters with John Reed and Brocklehurst, Brontë again makes the association of sex and literal death. Rochester's love song to Jane intimates they will die together. Jane replies, "What did he mean by such a pagan idea? *I* had no intention of dying with him—he might depend on that" (344). Bertha's fate will confirm Jane's fear: Rochester paradoxically becomes both rescuer and killer as, in his very efforts to save Bertha, he precipitates her suicidal leap into the flames.

Virginia Woolf, too, saw Rochester as a figure of devastation, attributing his characterization to Brontë's own personal suffering. Woolf writes in *A Room of One's Own*:

> The portrait of Rochester is drawn in the dark. We feel the influence of fear in it; just as we constantly feel an acidity [in Brontë] which is the result of oppression, a buried suffering smouldering beneath her passion, a rancour which contracts these books, spendid as they are, with a spasm of pain.[13]

Brontë fears for Jane's psychological survival as she apparently feared for her own, as is indicated in a letter written to her friend Ellen Nussey:

> My good girl, "une grande passion" is "une grande folie" ... no young lady should fall in love till the offer has been made, accepted—the marriage ceremony performed and the first half year of wedded life has passed away—a woman may then begin to love, but with great precaution—very coldly—very moderately—very rationally—if she ever loves so much that a harsh word or a cold look from her husband cuts her to the heart— she is a fool—if ever she loves so much that her husband's will is her law—and that she has got into the habit of watching his looks in order that she may anticipate his wishes, she will soon be a neglected fool.[14]

It is possible that Rochester's need to reduce Jane to the state of object indicates an insecurity of his own. Jane's very virginity and inexperience are perhaps the qualities which most attract Rochester because he perceives them to be those most opposite to Bertha's. Bertha's sexuality, her capacity for passion, apparently presented Rochester with real difficulties. Bertha possessed, Rochester tells Jane, "neither modesty, nor benevolence, nor candour, nor refinement in her mind or manners" (389). She was "coarse and trite, perverse and imbecile" (390). "Her vices sprang up fast and rank," and she demonstrated "giant propensities," being "intemperate and unchaste." Her nature was "the most gross, impure, depraved I ever saw" (391). Rochester comes to despise Bertha's very geographical origin, its lush, tropical refulgence being associated with her sexual personality.

Adrienne Rich, in an article entitled *"Jane Eyre*: Temptations of a Motherless Woman," provides a possible explanation for Rochester's attitude toward his wife:

> The 19th century loose woman might have sexual feelings, but the 19th century *wife* did not and must not. Rochester's loathing of Bertha is described repeatedly in terms of her physical strength and her violent will—both unacceptable qualities in the 19th century female, raised to the nth degree and embodied in a monster.[15]

Rochester further inadvertently reveals what might be seen as his own sexual inadequacy as he explains to Jane his chain of mistresses: "I tried dissipation—never debauchery: that I hated, and hate" (397). Moglen's psychosexual analysis of the Byronic hero in general is illuminating in Rochester's case: "Always intrinsically connected to man's insecurity concerning his own sexuality, the fear of women is particularly pronounced in \sychology of the Byronic hero whose need to prove his masculinity by sexual conquest drives him to extremes of behavior."[16]

To preserve his own sexual identity, Rochester must rob Jane of hers. He insists on associating Jane with the supernatural rather than with the natural, that is, the sexual. He refers to her repeatedly as "angel," "fairy," "elf," "spirit," and tells little Adele that he will take Mademoiselle to the moon to live in an alabaster cave. Even Adele is skeptical, knowing that a real Jane is preferable to an idealized image. Rochester also emphasizes the contrast between Jane and Bertha, the purity of one and what he sees as the result of gross sexuality in the other, as he calls upon assembled wedding guests to witness his justification for bigamy:

> That is *my wife*. . . . And *this* is what I wished to have . . . this young girl, who stands so grave and quiet at the mouth of hell, looking collectedly at the gambols of a demon. I wanted her just as a change after that fierce ragout . . . look at the difference! Compare these clear eyes with the red balls yonder—this face with that mask—this form with that bulk. . . . (371)

Bertha at this point, however, can hardly be seen as a sexual being, her very sexual identity having been lost with her claim to humanity. Jane later accuses Rochester: "You are inexorable for that unfortunate lady: you speak of her with hate—with vindictive antipathy. It is cruel—she cannot help being mad." Rochester counters, "If you were mad, do you think I should hate you?" and Jane responds, "I do indeed, sir" (384).

Nearly as complex and dangerous as Rochester is St. John Rivers, the clergyman master of Moor's End, yet another female community. St. John's masculine attractiveness, like Rochester's, poses a temptation for a sexually deprived Jane:

> I can imagine the possibility of conceiving an inevitable, strange, torturing kind of love for him: because he is so

talented; and there is often a certain heroic grandeur in
his look, manner, and conversation (531).

But she also knows, from previous experience and from
intuition, that love threatens the self:

> In that case, my lot would become unspeakably
> wretched. He would not want me to love him; and if I
> showed the feeling, he would make me sensible that it
> was a superfluity. . . . It is better, therefore, for the insig-
> nificant to keep out of his way; lest, in his progress, he
> should trample them down (531).

St. John, like his predecessors, is seen as a potential
murderer, both of the mind and of the body. On a literal level, St. John seeks to lead Jane to a missionary life
in India, a place of such extreme climate, Jane feels, as
to assure her an early death. "God did not give me my
life to throw away," she tells St. John, "and to do as you
wish me would, I begin to think, be almost equivalent to
committing suicide" (528).

At the same time that he wishes to burn her body in
India, St. John wishes to freeze her soul by denying her
physical love. In his stern Calvinism, reminiscent of
Brocklehurst's, St. John would deny Jane's sexual and
human self by binding her in a loveless and passion-
less marriage. "Would it not be strange," Jane asks
herself, "to be chained for life to a man who regarded
one but as a useful tool?" (531) As the predominant
image for Rochester is fire, so St. John is associated with
ice—both extremes threaten death or the loss of identity, sexual and psychological.

The slave image becomes associated with St. John as it
has with other male characters. "His kiss was like a seal
affixed to my fetters," Jane says (509). And again: "By
degrees, he acquired a certain influence over me that
took away my liberty of mind" (508). St. John, like
Rochester, is seen in fact as threatening the self with
engulfment:

> I was tempted to cease struggling with him—to rush
> down the torrent of his will into the gulf of his existence,
> and there lose my own. I was almost as hard beset by him
> now as I had been once before, in a different way, by
> another. I was a fool both times (534).

Pushed to the extreme by St. John's insistence on marriage, Jane cries out, "If I were to marry you, you would kill me. You are killing me now" (526). St. John, reflecting his society's attitude that woman's role is to surrender to the male will, reproves Jane: "Your words are such as ought not to be used—they are violent, unfeminine. . . ." (526–27)

These very charges are those brought repeatedly against Bertha Mason. Critics have frequently seen her as "unfeminine"—as either androgynous or as a kind of parody of masculinity. Terry Eagleton in his study of the Brontës, for example, sees Bertha partly as a projection of Jane's psyche, yet, "since Bertha is masculine, black-visaged and almost the same height as her husband, she appears also as a repulsive symbol of Rochester's sexual drive."[17] Moglen, for another, describes Bertha in this way: ". . . an androgynous figure, she is also the violent lover who destroys the integrity of the self; who offers the corruption of sexual knowledge and power—essentially male in its opposition to purity and innocence."[18]

Certainly Bertha's violent behavior—rending male antagonists with her very teeth—can be called "unfeminine." She has not, however, been masculinized, but rather desexed altogether, symbolically castrated in the same way that Jane's sexual self has been repeatedly threatened by Rochester and others. Bertha's opposition to "purity and innocence," too, is questionable. It is worthy of note that she attacks male figures, never her female keeper, Grace Poole, or Jane, though she enters Jane's room and leans above her sleeping form. It is on this night that Bertha tears Jane's wedding veil, which Jane herself has said is a symbol of "nothing save Fairfax Rochester's pride" (355). Finally, Bertha is the agent for Rochester's purification as well as his fall.

Perhaps Bertha's madness quite literally has a method, and, as Grace Poole has said, "it is not in mortal discretion to fathom her craft" (370). She behaves in such an "unfeminine" manner as many "feminine" people, like Jane herself, might find possible only in fantasy. Perhaps Brontë even suggests, with the depiction of the ebony crucifix on the cabinet door which hides the entrance to Bertha's den, an identification with the scapegoat aspect of the dying Christ (264).

But such an identification for Bertha is, at best, tenuous and possibly subconscious on Brontë's part. The figure of Bertha is, after all, a warning and not a model. A more sympathetic view of Bertha and a reinterpretation of her insanity occur in Jean Rhys's novel *Wide Sargasso Sea*.[19] Rhys has rewritten the mad sequences from *Jane Eyre* from Bertha's point of view, allowing her to tell her own story from the account of her childhood in the West Indies through her marriage to Rochester and her eventual breakdown and confinement at Thornfield Hall. Rhys's Bertha, unlike Brontë's, is delicate in her appearance and feminine in her behavior. Even the name "Bertha," declared to be solely Rochester's appellation for her, is changed to the more musical "Antoinette." Rhys also dismisses the allegations made by Brontë's Rochester that Bertha's insanity is hereditary, and provides excellent alternative causes for both Antoinette's and her mother's psychoses. The mother has suffered a series of atrocities during a native uprising; Antoinette has undergone Rochester's prudish and cruel rejection of her passion for him. Rhys's Rochester is the unmitigated villain as he consciously inflicts the most insidious forms of mental torture.

In her imprisonment at Thornfield Hall, Antoinette
is more pathetic than bestial, her periods of violence
clouded by amnesia so that we never see her at her
worst. She becomes more and more the lost child, the
wronged innocent. Her fault, however, is the same as
that of Brontë's Bertha—she has unreservedly surrendered to her passion for Rochester. Rhys's character,
then, shares with Brontë's this basic similarity: they are
both vehicles for the essentially feminist message that,
whatever the sexual ethos, there is a danger of the loss
of self when self-love and self-preservation become sec-
ondary to love for another.

In Brontë's novel Jane first sees Bertha's face reflected in a mirror, and a wall, after all, is all that separates Jane from Bertha in the setting for one of Brontë's
most overtly feminist and didactic statements. Jane, like
her double, paces the third floor of Thornfield Hall,
longing for some unnameable form of liberty, experiencing a "restlessness" which would be deemed im-
proper, even irrational, for the Victorian woman:

> Who blames me? Many no doubt; and I shall be called
> discontented. I could not help it: the restlessness was in
> my nature; it agitated me to pain sometimes. Then my
> sole relief was to walk along the corridor of the third
> story, backwards and forwards. . . .
> It is vain to say human beings ought to be satisfied with
> tranquility: they must have action; and they will make it
> if they cannot find it. Millions are condemned to a stiller
> doom than mine, and millions are in silent revolt against
> their lot. Nobody knows how many rebellions besides
> political rebellions ferment in the masses of life which
> people earth. Women are supposed to be very calm gen-
> erally: but women feel just as men feel; they need exer-
> cise for their faculties, and a field for their efforts as
> much as their brothers do; they suffer from too rigid a
> restraint, too absolute a stagnation, precisely as men
> would suffer; and it is narrow-minded in their more
> privileged fellow-creatures to say that they ought to con-

fine themselves to making purses and knitting stockings, to playing on the piano and embroidering bags. It is thoughtless to condemn them, or laugh at them, if they seek to do more or learn more than custom has pronounced necessary for their sex (132–33).

The next lines, which so disturbed Virginia Woolf in her reading of *Jane Eyre* and left her at a loss for explanation,[20] describe the laugh of the lunatic in close proximity: "the same peal, the same low, slow ha! ha! which, when first heard, had thrilled me" (133). Bertha, herself one of the "millions fermenting rebellion," longing for "action," and quite obviously suffering from "too rigid a restraint," perhaps laughs, along with Brontë herself, at Jane's naive understatement.

It is a similar kind of undefined restlessness to that Jane experiences which precipitates the temporary insanity of Lucy Snowe, the protagonist of Brontë's *Villette*, a novel which Kate Millett in *Sexual Politics* describes as "too subversive to be popular."[21] Lucy is alone in a girls' school which has been abandoned for the summer vacation when she begins to experience extreme depression, "the conviction that fate was of stone, and Hope a false idol—blind, bloodless, and of granite core."[22] Terrible dreams, Lucy says, "wring my whole frame with unknown anguish" and provide "a nameless experience that had the hue, the mien, the terror, the very tone of a visitation from eternity." Such dreams lead her to the realization that "my mind has suffered somewhat too much; a malady is growing upon it—what shall I do? How shall I keep well?"[23] Lucy, like Jane, does keep well, but only by an exertion of will and an affirmation of the self as indomitable. Kate Millett describes her in this way: "In Lucy one may perceive what effects her life in a male-supremacist society has upon the psyche of a woman. She is bitter and she is honest; a neurotic revolutionary full of conflict, back-sliding, anger, terrible self-doubt, and an unconquerable determination to win through."[24]

Like Lucy, and like Bertha, Jane is, when driven, capable of "unfeminine" outbursts of temper and even of violence, and in these acts, at least partly, lie her survival. The Victorian adjuration to the female, "suffer and be still," is to Brontë's mind yet another weapon of patriarchal domination. Jane has, after all, punched John Reed, and she has told the subservient Helen Burns:

> If people were always kind and obedient to those who are cruel and unjust, the wicked people would have it all their own way: they would never feel afraid, and so they would never alter, but would grow worse and worse. When we are struck at without reason, we should strike back again very hard; I am sure we should—so hard as to teach the person who struck us never to do it again (65).

The adult Jane has hardly changed:

> I know no medium: I never in my life have known any medium in my dealings with positive, hard characters, antagonistic to my own, between absolute submission and determined revolt. I have always faithfully observed the one, up to the very moment of bursting, sometimes with volcanic vehemence, into the other.... (511)

Laing's observations on the feelings of the ontologically threatened person are perhaps relevant here. Hate, says Laing, can be a less disturbing relationship than love because it is somehow less engulfing. Liking a person, Laing writes in *The Divided Self*, can be equal to being *like* that person, or even being the *same* as that person, thus with losing one's own identity. Hating and being hated may therefore be interpreted as less threatening to the sense of self.[25]

Margot Peters, in her biography, remarks on Brontë's own capacity for intense resentment and hatred. Peters quotes Brontë's self-description written in a letter to

Ellen Nussey: "I am a hearty hater."²⁶ Certainly, within
the scope of her novel, Brontë is capable of great ven-
geance. In order to preserve Jane's self from annihilation, Brontë annihilates the oppressors, systematically
and thoroughly. John Reed dies a suicide as a result of
his own excesses; Brocklehurst is socially discredited
and disappears; and St. John, at the novel's end, is soon
to find his martyrdom in death. These characters have
been rendered strawmen by Jane's assertion of self.

Perhaps the greatest victory is that achieved over
Rochester. Jane clearly surpasses her statement (which
is also something of a threat) made earlier in the novel:

> I have as much soul as you,—and full as much heart!
> And if God had gifted me with some beauty, and much
> wealth, I should have made it as hard for you to leave
> me, as it is now for me to leave you . . . it is my spirit that
> addresses your spirit; just as if both had passed through
> the grave, and we stood at God's feet, equal,—as we are!
> (318)

Such a claim to equality, addressed in the Victorian age
to a male and a male employer at that, is surely insurrec-
tion.

Ultimately, however, as Jane seeks out Rochester in
the final chapters to find his house in ruins, his body
crippled and blinded, his worst fears realized in the de-
pletion of his powers of masculinity, she finds herself his
superior rather than his equal. Rochester has leaned on
Jane before: at their first meeting when he falls from his
horse, later when Bertha sets fire to his bed, and at
other intervals of crisis. Now he must formally avow his
dependence, "just as if a royal eagle, chained to a perch,
should be forced to entreat a sparrow to become its
purveyor" (562). Significantly, Rochester now bestows
on Jane his watch and chain, that very chain to which he
had threatened to attach her during their earlier relationship.

Moglen maintains that, like Brontë's own blinded father whom she nursed as she wrote *Jane Eyre*, Rochester, at the end of the novel, is in need of a mother—not a lover. Jane can assume the role of what Moglen terms "the virginal daughter who has been magically transformed—without the mediation of sexual contact—into the noble figure of the nurturing mother."[27]

Carolyn Heilbrun in *Toward a Recognition of Androgyny* provides a purely political interpretation of Rochester's fall:

> Jane Eyre's demand for autonomy or some measure of freedom echoes politically in the cries of all powerless individuals whether the victims of industrialization, racial discrimination or political disenfranchisement. So we today begin to see that Rochester undergoes, not sexual mutilation as the Freudians claim, but the inevitable sufferings necessary when those in power are forced to release some of their power to those who previously had none.[28]

Whether sexual, political, or psychological, it is a terrible justice which Brontë calls down upon Rochester. "My master" has become "my Edward" and Jane can aggressively announce, "Reader, I married him" (574).

More important than the victories over the male oppressors, and more difficult for Brontë, is the annihilation of the insane doppelgänger, the potential Jane-as-victim. She must be done away with both physically and as a shadow in the mind. Metaphors associating passion with madness, both of which Brontë sees as a loss of self and sexual identity, recur throughout the novel. Early in her relationship with Rochester, Jane warns herself that

> it is madness in all women to let a secret love kindle within them, which, if unreturned and unknown, must devour the life that feeds it; and if discovered and re-

sponded to, must lead, *ignis fatuus*-like, into miry wilds
whence there is no extrication (201).

In a world so dangerous to the sanity, so oppressive to
the sense of self, one means of survival lies in being
inaccessible; and chastity is a form of inaccessibility.
Jane thus rejects the temptation to become Rochester's
mistress:

> I will keep the law given by God; sanctioned by man. I
> will hold to the principles received by men when I was
> sane, and not mad—as I am now. . . . If I cannot believe it
> now, it is because I am insane—quite insane: with my
> veins running fire, and my heart beating faster than I
> can count its throbs. Preconceived opinions, foregone
> determinations, are all I have at this hour to stand by:
> there I plant my foot (404–5).

Peters describes Jane's chastity as "the source of that
self-esteem which can keep her alive."[29] Jane celebrates
her own physical and psychological survival:

> . . . let me ask myself one question—which is better?—to
> have surrendered to temptation; listened to passion;
> made no painful effort—no struggle;—but to have sunk
> down in the silken snare; fallen asleep on the flowers
> covering it. . . Whether is it better, I ask, to be a slave in a
> fool's paradise at Marseilles—fevered with delusive bliss
> one hour—suffocating with the bitterest tears of remorse
> and shame the next—or to be a village-schoolmistress,
> free and honest, in a breezy mountain nook in the
> healthy heart of England?
> Yes; I feel now that I was right when I adhered to
> principle and law, and scorned and crushed the insane
> promptings of a frenzied moment (459).

Chastity, which Brontë often euphemizes as the "un-
mined treasure" of the body, and sanity, the mind's
treasure, thus become synonomous.

In thus asserting chastity and self, rejecting the self-
abnegating role traditional for women, Jane also rejects
the authority of the male power structure. She seeks,

throughout the novel, another kind of authority—that
of the female. Adrienne Rich has suggested that *Jane
Eyre* is the story of a search for a literal mother:

> Many of the great mothers have not been biological. The
> novel *Jane Eyre* ... can be read as a woman-pilgrim's
> progress along a path of classic female temptation, in
> which the motherless Jane time after time finds women
> who protect, solace, teach, challenge, and nourish her in
> self-respect. For centuries, daughters have been
> strengthened and energized by nonbiological mothers,
> who have combined a care for the practical values of
> survival with an incitement toward further horizons, a
> compassion for vulnerability with an insistence on our
> buried strengths. It is precisely this that has allowed us to
> survive. . . .[30]

The fact that Brontë, like Jane, was motherless lends a
poignancy to this search for an actual, literal mother
figure. However, unlike Rich, I feel that, within the
scope of the novel, such a search is doomed to disap-
pointment. There is hardly a female character in Jane's
acquaintance who has not conformed in some way to
social expectations for the female. Mrs. Reed, whose
energies are consumed in pampering her son, rejects
Jane and chooses to assume the role of evil stepmother
rather than provide Jane with the nurturing love she
longs for. On the occasion of Mrs. Reed's death, later in
the novel, Jane reveals: "Many a time, as a little child, I
should have been glad to love you if you would have let
me" (300). Jane finds some grudging affection,
motivated undoubtedly by pity, in the person of Bessie,
the maid, whose song of "The Poor Orphan Child,"
however, serves only to confirm Jane's sense of loss. At
Lowood Institution, Jane seeks love and tenderness with
Helen Burns, but Helen is solipsistically caught up in
her own vision of Christian stoicism and dies a martyr of
self-denial, an act which Jane's strong survival instincts
would never permit her to emulate. Miss Temple, the

beloved teacher, also in effect abandons Jane when she leaves Lowood to marry a respectable clergyman. Diana and Mary Rivers, the sisters of St. John, arrive on the scene only after they are no longer needed as mother figures, and they too marry and are lost to Jane.

The only mother available to Jane is thus a metaphoric mother, virtually a cosmic force, who lives both in the universe and in the self. Jane sees her clearly for the first time on the night of her abortive wedding to Rochester. She lies alone in her room at Thornfield, as desperately unhappy as she had been in the red room at Gateshead, where there also occurred revelations of a quasi-supernatural nature. Now Jane communicates with the moon itself:

> She broke forth as never moon yet burst from cloud: a hand first penetrated the sable folds and waved them away; then, not a moon, but a white human form shone in the azure, inclining a glorious brow earthward. It gazed and gazed on me. It spoke to my spirit: immeasurably distant was the tone, yet so near, it whispered in my heart—
> "My daughter, flee temptation!"
> "Mother, I will" (407).

The moon here undoubtedly represents, in accordance with long literary tradition, primarily chastity. Yet Bronte's images are never quite so simple. For example, a similar moon often precedes the apparition of the nun in *Villette* whose mysterious life had included some sin, presumably sexual, against her vows. Perhaps Brontë would be more in accord with the Jungian psychologist M. Esther Harding, who devotes her study *Woman's Mysteries* to an analysis of the moon-mother in ancient and modern cultures. Various moon goddesses, says Harding, have represented fertility as well as chastity; they are universally autoerotic, "one-in-themselves," belonging only to themselves.[31] If we can assume such a complexity for Brontë's image, it is possible to conclude that the moon-mother is the voice of the feminist conscious-ness, a kind of inner voice of sanity which, unlike the traditional patriarchal God to whom Jane frequently pays lip service, affirms self-respect and not self-denial, sexual or otherwise.

Again, as Jane wanders the moors in flight from Rochester, she finds affinity with the cosmic mother rather than with the male God. This time the mother-goddess is represented by the earth rather than by the moon:

> I have no relative but the universal mother, Nature: I will seek her breast and ask repose. . . . Nature seemed to me benign and good; I thought she loved me, outcast as I was; and I, who from man could anticipate only mistrust, rejection, insult, clung to her with filial fondness. To-night, at least, I would be her guest—as I was her child: my mother would lodge me without money and without price (412–13).

Jane is thus so absorbed in her own search for the mother that she at least subconsciously rejects the role of motherhood for herself as being yet another threat to autonomy. Though the novel abounds in images of pregnancy and conception, as Peters has pointed out in *Style in the Novel*,[32] Brontë spares but a few lines for the birth of Jane's own child. We know only that it is a male child who has inherited Rochester's black eyes. Jane's attitude toward Adele has been one of professional in-dulgence rather than sincere affection, and shortly after Jane's marriage to Rochester Adele is unceremoniously shipped off to school. Also reflective of Jane's reluc-tance to assume the role of mother herself is her recur-ring dream of the wailing infant which clings to her neck, strangles her at times, poses a terrifying responsi-bility in the form of a burden which she is not permitted to lay down, and always forbodes disaster. That which at least partly contributes to Lucy Snowe's mental crisis in *Villette* is her onerous duty as sole caretaker of an idiot child. Moglen attributes such feelings of obvious antipathy to the fact that Brontë's own mother died very probably as the result of excessive child bearing.[33] Ironically, Brontë herself was to die of complications of pregnancy.

Thus, Jane wishes only to be a mother to her *self*, and the authority she has sought in the moon and in the earth is after all but the mother within. Jane, at a moment of severe temptation, asks herself, "Who in the world cares for *you*?" Her immediate recognition is, "*I* care for myself. The more solitary, the more friendless, the more unsustained I am, the more I will respect myself" (404). The female self, for Brontë, is an idea of psychological order; its preservation lies in the sanity of the feminist consciousness.

2

"The Sane and the Insane": *Psychosis and Mysticism in* Mrs. Dalloway

Much madness is divinest sense
To a discerning eye;
Much sense the starkest madness.
Tis the majority
In this, as all, prevails.
Assent, and you are sane;
Demur,—you're straightway dangerous,
And handled with a chain.

Emily Dickinson

"I ADUMBRATE HERE a study of insanity and suicide; the world seen by the sane and the insane side by side,"[1] wrote Virginia Woolf of her projected novel *Mrs. Dalloway*. Unlike Brontë's clear-cut distinction between sanity and psychosis in a society in which psychological survival is at least a desirable possibility, Woolf's dividing line is an extremely fine one, obscured in a world in which insanity may well be a "sane" alternative.

Like Brontë, and like Lessing, to be explored in the next chapter, Woolf juxtaposes her "sane" character to an insane doppelgänger: Clarissa Dalloway represents the "normally" alienated person who functions in her society, but whose other and perhaps better self is the madman Septimus Warren Smith. As has been noted in most critical studies of *Mrs. Dalloway*, the two characters are linked structurally by a series of words and phrases which pervade the interior monologues of both. Sea, waves, drowning, fire, trees, flowers, "fear no more" are all recurring images for both characters. Although they never meet, their paths through the physical world cross throughout the novel. On another level, the basis of their connection would also seem to be the experiences of both, differing only in degree of intensity, in the subjective realms of anxiety, isolation, ontological insecurity, and, finally, psychosis and mysticism.

41

On the first page of *Mrs. Dalloway* we are told that Clarissa, as a girl, was often preoccupied with the feeling that "something awful was about to happen."[2] Her sense of nameless anxiety and her feelings of isolation become thematic in the novel: "She had a perpetual sense . . . of being out, out, far out to sea and alone; she always had the feeling that it was very, very dangerous to live even one day" (11). For Septimus, the dread of impending disaster is even more intense. "The world has raised its whip; where will it descend?" (20). There is always, in the consciousness of Septimus, "something tremendous about to happen" (104).

Given her presentation of the world, Woolf might well see these anxieties as justified, as projections of minds which are hyperperceptive of a bizarre reality. As in the foregoing chapter, the ideas of R. D. Laing serve to illuminate the nature of this reality. In *The Politics of Experience*, for example, Laing quotes a phrase from Heidegger which echoes Woolf: "The Dreadful has already happened"; that is, society itself has become a composition of individuals who are what Laing calls "sane-schizoids," people alienated from their own inner selves and therefore isolated from each other as well.[3] Woolf, like Brontë, sees sexual oppression as symptomatic of the illness of such a society. Thus, although many critics describe Clarissa and Septimus as linked by a common attribute of androgyny, they may also be seen, in their relationship to society, as essentially "feminine" in that both are victimized, to varying extents, by a male-supremacist system.

While Brontë portrays the individual male as negative authority figure, Woolf, in *Mrs. Dalloway* and even more obviously in later works, depicts a universalized vision of virility manifesting itself, ultimately, as fascism. Its victims are those members of humanity who are powerless, "feminine" men as well as women. Woolf describes her "mental picture" in *Three Guineas,* published as Hitler was moving through Europe:

> It is the figure of a man; some say, others deny, that he is Man himself, the quintessence of virility, the perfect type of which all others are imperfect adumbrations. He is a man certainly. His eyes are glazed; his eyes glare. His body, which is braced in an unnatural position, is tightly cased in a uniform. Upon the breast of that uniform are sewn several medals and other mystic symbols. His hand is upon the sword. He is called in German and Italian Fuhrer or Duce; in our own language Tyrant or Dictator. And behind him lie ruined houses and dead bodies— men, women and children.[4]

Although E. M. Forster prejudicially describes *Three Guineas* as "cantankerous" and Woolf's feminism as "old fashioned,"[5] his evaluation of her attitude toward society is accurate if patronizing:

> She was convinced that society is man-made, that the chief occupations of men are the shedding of blood, the making of money, the giving of orders, and the wearing of uniforms, and that none of these occupations is admirable.[6]

Woolf maintains throughout *Three Guineas* that the public world is but a reflection of the private world, that the system which approves tyranny of women in the home will also condone the tyranny of humanity in general. Thus, Woolf sees little distinction between feminism and humanism.

War, as a weapon of tyranny and as a manifestation of that "quintessence of virility," is an ominous presence in all Woolf's novels, including *Mrs. Dalloway*. Septimus is diagnosed as suffering from "deferred shell shock," his very mind being a casualty of war. Alex Zwerdling, in his article "*Mrs. Dalloway* and the Social System," interprets Septimus's condition as "a psychic wound from which he has no wish to recover because it is a badge of honor in a society that identifies composure with mental health."[7] But society itself in *Mrs. Dalloway* does not reflect any real composure; it is rather an active and malignant force. Woolf states in her diary, "I want to criticize the social system, and to show it at work, at its most intense."[8]

Woolf's personification of this social system is the famed psychiatrist Sir William Bradshaw, a warrior against the forces of irrationality and a hero to his countrymen:

> Worshipping proportion, Sir William not only prospered himself but made England prosper, secluded her lunatics, forbade childbirth, penalised despair, made it impossible for the unfit to propagate their views until they, too, shared his sense of proportion ... insisting that these prophetic Christs and Christesses, who prophesied the end of the world, or the advent of God, should drink milk in bed, as Sir William ordered; Sir William with his thirty years' experience of these kinds of cases, and his infallible instinct, this is madness, this sense; in fact, his sense of proportion (150–51).

> Naked, defenceless, the exhausted, the friendless received the impress of Sir William's will. He swooped, he devoured, he shut people up (154).

Thus, for both Woolf and Septimus, Sir William is the powerful representative of the masculine aspect of human nature, "the brute with the red nostrils" (223). Clarissa, too, imagines what destruction might occur if Sir William were to have access to the mind, the authority to penetrate the self. She muses on Septimus's suicide, of which she has just been informed, and she knows intuitively just how tragically Bradshaw has mishandled Septimus's condition:

> Or there were the poets and thinkers. Suppose he had had that passion, and had gone to Sir William Bradshaw, a great doctor yet to her obscurely evil, without sex or lust, extremely polite to women, but capable of some

> indescribable outrage—forcing your soul, that was it—if
> this young man had gone to him, and Sir William had
> impressed him, like that, with his power, might he not
> then have said (indeed she felt it now), Life is made
> intolerable; they make life intolerable, men like that?
> (281)

Sir William's sexually threatening presence recalls Brontë's characterization of the Reverend Brocklehurst and, to some extent, her depiction of St. John Rivers. All three figures are presented as excessively masculine, yet all are, paradoxically, "without sex," forbidding natural sexual expression in others. All are cold, inhuman themselves—and thus terrifying. Brocklehurst and Sir William are tyrants. Brocklehurst's long, accusing finger becomes, in the case of Sir William, a gesture prophetically like the fascist salute. His patients cower as

> they learnt the extent of their transgressions; huddled
> up in armchairs, they watched him go through, for their
> benefit, a curious exercise with the arms, which he shot
> out, brought sharply back to his hip, to prove (if the
> patient was obstinate) that Sir William was master of his
> own actions, which the patient was not. There some
> weakly broke down; sobbed, submitted; others inspired
> by Heaven knows what intemperate madness, called Sir
> William to his face a damnable humbug; questioned,
> even more impiously, life itself. Why live? they de-
> manded. Sir William replied that life was good (153).

Society in *Mrs. Dalloway* produces many such examples of excessive dominance, though not all are so pervasively powerful as Sir William, and not all are men. For example, Miss Kilman, as her name indicates, seeks to annihilate the individualized self of others with her fanatic political and religious proselytizing and with her possessive lesbian yearnings. Her obscene pleasure in grossly fingering and sucking the very marrow from a chocolate eclair indicates her will to treat persons in a similar fashion. Clarissa perceives her in threatening

sexual terms as "one of those spectres who stand astride
us and suck up half our life-blood, dominators and tyrants" (16–17).

Individuals, whether men or masculinized women
like Miss Kilman, are not the only assailants in Woolf's
dangerous universe; at times the very atmosphere of
London becomes profoundly threatening. Septimus
stands helplessly watching:

> In the street, vans roared past him; brutality blared out
> on placards; men were trapped in mines; women burnt
> alive; and once a maimed file of lunatics being exercised
> or displayed for the diversion of the populace (who
> laughed aloud), ambled and nodded and grinned past
> him, in the Tottenham Court Road, each half apologeti-
> cally, yet triumphantly, inflicting his helpless woe. And
> would *he* go mad? (135–36)

The world is thus perceived by both Clarissa and Septimus as threatening to one's individuality, one's sense
of the self. There are, however, defensive mechanisms
which can be adopted to preserve the sense of self, to
achieve a measure of ontological security. When taken
to their logical conclusion, they represent insanity, as in
the case of Septimus. But Clarissa, too, though to a less
drastic extent, employs the same methods.

Because the apprehension of their surroundings is so
sensitive, so painful, both Clarissa and Septimus, on an
unconscious or even a conscious level, refuse to "feel."
They perceive themselves as empty, lacking, for example, in the ability to relate to other people. Although
Clarissa is not only a part but a very center of society,
she rejects close personal contacts. Other women "con-
fess" to Clarissa, but never Clarissa to them. She "could
see what she lacked ... it was something central which
permeated; something warm which broke up surfaces
and rippled the cold contact of man and woman, or of

women together" (46). She observes, "There was an emptiness about the heart of life" (45).

Septimus, even more consistently and intensely, repeats that he cannot feel, that he is empty; he wishes himself a shell of a whole person. "His wife was crying, and he felt nothing; only each time she sobbed in this profound, this silent, this hopeless way, he descended another step into the pit" (136).

Laing's definition of schizophrenia, explored in *The Divided Self*, applies quite clearly to Septimus and, to a degree, to Clarissa as well:

> The term schizoid refers to an individual the totality of whose experience is split in two main ways: in the first place, there is a rent in his relationship with his world, and, in the second, there is a disruption of his relationship with himself. Such a person is not able to experience himself "together with" others or "at home in" the world, but, on the contrary, he experiences himself in despairing aloneness and isolation. . . . [9]

What Woolf perceives in *Mrs. Dalloway* and what Laing is later to plead in *The Politics of Experience* is that, if the world is in truth inhospitable, unhomelike, then perhaps withdrawal from that world is a sane and reasonable method of self-preservation.

That social institution in which the self is most vulnerable because most intimate with another is, of course, marriage. Given Woolf's frequent connection of private and public tyranny, it is not surprising, for example, that the public tyrant Sir William Bradshaw most especially does not spare his own wife, who, however, has proved a willing victim:

> But conversion, fastidious Goddess, loves blood better than brick, and feasts most subtly on the human will. For example, Lady Bradshaw. Fifteen years ago she had gone under. It was nothing you could put your finger on; there had been no scene, no snap; only the slow

> sinking, water-logged, of her will into his. Sweet was her
> smile, swift her submission. . . . (152)

Clarissa refuses such victimization. Her early suitor, Peter Walsh, has posed a similar if more subtle threat to psychological security. Very like Mr. Ramsay, the often tyrannical husband in *To the Lighthouse* whose military-like boots become a symbol of negative masculinity, Peter is also excessively masculine as evidenced by his ever-present phallic pen-knife. Clarissa reaffirms her rejection of Peter and her reasons for marrying Richard Dalloway instead:

> So she would still find herself arguing in St. James's Park, still making out that she had been right—and she had too—not to marry him. For in marriage a little license, a little independence there must be between people living together day in and day out in the same house; which Richard gave her and she him. . . . But with Peter everything had to be shared; everything gone into. And it was intolerable, and when it came to that scene in the little garden by the fountain, she had to break with him or they would have been destroyed, both of them ruined, she was convinced (10).

Later in the novel, Clarissa again considers:

> And there is a dignity in people; a solitude; even between husband and wife a gulf; and that one must respect, thought Clarissa, watching him open the door; for one would not part with it oneself, or take it, against his will, from one's husband, without losing one's independence, one's self-respect—something, after all, priceless (181).

Such privacy is a paramount value for all Woolf's sympathetic, that is "feminine," characters. Mrs. Ramsay in *To the Lighthouse*, we begin to feel, dies for the lack of it. Septimus, ultimately, commits suicide to achieve it. Woolf wrote in an essay entitled "On Being Ill":

> We do not know our own souls, let alone the souls of
> others. Human beings do not go hand in hand the whole
> stretch of the way. There is a virgin forest in each; a
> snowfield where even the print of birds' feet is unknown.
> Here we go alone, and like it better so. Always to have
> sympathy, always to be accompanied, always to be un-
> derstood would be intolerable.[10]

Even marriage to Richard, however, who permits
Clarissa this precious privacy and agrees that she sleep
alone, is not without danger. "She had the oddest sense
of being herself invisible; unseen; unknown... this
being Mrs. Dalloway; not even Clarissa any more; this
being Mrs. Richard Dalloway" (14). A similar fear, that
of losing one's identity with one's name in marriage, is
also expressed in *Jane Eyre* and, as we will see, preoc-
cupies Lessing in *The Four-Gated City*.

Woolf, like Brontë, sees a necessity to protect the self
by withdrawing, by being inaccessible, in the area of
sexual relationships. Clarissa, like Jane Eyre, is frequently depicted as virginal, even nunlike, and, like
Jane, she is ambivalent, longing for love and yet rejecting it because of its dangers. Clarissa perceives clearly
that she has left the sexual, fertile life for the tower,
where security is possible but where isolation and death
are juxtaposed images:

> It was all over for her. The sheet was stretched and the
> bed narrow. She had gone into the tower alone and left
> them blackberrying in the sun. The door had shut, and
> there among the dust of fallen plaster and the litter of
> birds' nests, how distant the view had looked, and the
> sounds came thin and chill.... (70)

(Surely the inaccessible lighthouse in *To the Lighthouse*
represents a similar, longed-for isolation for Mrs. Ramsay.)

Sex and love, for both Septimus and Clarissa as for

Jane Eyre, threaten a violation of the inner self which
one must struggle to keep intact. Clarissa agonizes to
herself:

> ... love and religion would destroy that, whatever it was,
> the privacy of the soul. ...
>   Love destroyed too. Everything that was fine, every-
> thing that was true went. ... Horrible passion! ... De-
> grading passion! (192)

Septimus, even more than Clarissa, is appalled by

> the getting of children, the sordidity of the mouth and
> the belly! ...
>   Love between man and woman was repulsive to
> Shakespeare. The business of copulation was filth to him
> before the end (134).

Hate, as in the case of Jane Eyre, becomes for Clarissa
and Septimus a less threatening, less engulfing emotion
than love. Clarissa, for example, finds great satisfaction
in her antipathy for Miss Kilman: "She hated her: she
loved her. It was enemies one wanted, not friends"
(266). Septimus is endowed with a great ability to love all
of humanity in spite of, or even because of, its faults, but
he also senses that "the secret signal which one genera-
tion passes, under disguise, to the next is loathing,
hatred, despair" (134). In his madness, Septimus perceives that "human beings have neither kindness, nor
faith, nor charity beyond what serves to increase the
pleasure of the moment. They hunt in packs. Their
packs scour the desert and vanish screaming into the
wilderness" (135).

Even Septimus's wife Rezia, who is the essence of positive femininity, surrounding herself with the feminine
symbol of flowers in her hatmaking trade, is not exempt
from Septimus's hatred. She inadvertently condemns
herself to loneliness and isolation from her husband by
her insistence on a "normal" marriage, which for her

includes children and sexual attention. She repeatedly "interrupts" (always a negative term in Woolf's novels), and thus destroys his visions by forcing him to see a reality he rejects. She rarely allows him the privacy which it costs him his sanity to achieve. Her ultimate betrayal is her allegiance to the doctors. Only too late does Rezia recognize Holmes and Bradshaw for the villains Woolf intends to portray. Always before fearful and birdlike, it is only in her last-minute attempt to protect Septimus from Holmes's violent entrance that she becomes strong and heroic, appearing then to Septimus as "a flowering tree," through the branches of which "looked out the face of a lawgiver, who had reached a sanctuary where she feared no one...." (224) After Septimus's death, Rezia comes to fully understand his visions as she too enters "into some garden" (227). She, like Septimus, hears and feels "rain falling, whisperings, stirrings among the dry corn, the caress of the sea...." (228)

The withdrawal from sexual relationships on the part of both Clarissa and Septimus has been explained by numerous critics, among whom is Nancy Topping Bazin in *Virginia Woolf and the Androgynous Vision*,[11] as a result of guilt due to repressed homosexual tendencies. Such tendencies do, of course, exist in both characters, but are more clearly explainable by the fact that each wishes to withdraw from what is perceived as a negative, masculine world in which the self can be theoretically violated sexually and psychologically, and to enter a feminine world of flower images and security. Clarissa, for example, is struck by "the purity, the integrity, of her feeling for Sally. It was not like one's feeling for a man. It was completely disinterested, and besides, it had a quality which could only exist between women" (50). Jane Eyre's search for the metaphoric mother involves a similar search for integrity rather than homosexual gratification. Certainly, a longing for immersion in the female world of Mrs. Ramsay is Lily Briscoe's object in *To the Lighthouse*. For Clarissa, however, such contacts are fleeting; there is always the male world to interrupt, to "embitter her moment of happiness.... It was like running one's face against a granite wall in the darkness!" (53)

In *Jane Eyre*, the price of sexual commitment is the loss of self in madness or death. Sexual love and passion are also dangerous in *Mrs. Dalloway*, but madness becomes a kind of refuge for the self rather than its loss. Septimus is, in a great sense, ultimately more victorious in his preservation of self than is Clarissa, who senses her relative failure. "A thing there was that mattered; a thing, wreathed about with chatter, defaced, obscured in her own life, let drop every day in corruption, lies, chatter. This he had preserved" (280).

The majority of Woolf scholars are in direct opposition to such a view. Jeremy Hawthorn, in *Virginia Woolf's Mrs. Dalloway*, for example, sees both Clarissa and Septimus as "impoverished" by what he terms sexual failure.[12] By cutting herself off from Peter Walsh, Hawthorn maintains, Clarissa "may have caused the death of her soul."[13] In general, Hawthorn perceives the great fault in *Mrs. Dalloway* as the lack of resolution of the sexual conflict and other problems: "We are led in this novel into the heart of the experience of human alienation, but we are not shown the way out, the way forward."[14] What especially mars Hawthorn's work is his naive mistaking of symptom for cause and his failure to see that, short of social revolution or the very regeneration of humanity itself, there simply *is* no way forward. In a male-supremacist society like that Woolf depicts, female ontology is in *fact* threatened. According to Laing, "a firm sense of one's own autonomous identity is required in order that one may be related as one human being to another."[15] When that sense of identity is continually threatened by social institutions as well as by individuals, its preservation reasonably lies in a withdrawal from danger.

Laing's theory that the ontologically threatened person experiences a sense of engulfment, or fear of the loss of one's identity in the identity of another,[16] applies to Woolf's novel as it does to Brontë's. The images of burning and drowning that appear so frequently in *Jane Eyre*, which Laing would see as expressive of this sense of engulfment, also recur throughout *Mrs. Dalloway*. Clarissa interrogates herself: "Why, after all, did she do these things? Why seek pinnacles and stand drenched in fire? Might it consume her anyhow! Burn her to cinders!" (255). For Septimus, such feelings occur with even greater frequency:

> Then there were the visions. He was drowned, he used to say, lying on a cliff with the gulls screaming over him. He would look over the edge of the sofa down into the sea.... And he would lie listening until suddenly he would cry that he was falling, down, down into the flames! (213)

The sense of engulfment, according to Laing, can be compounded by a fear of what he terms "implosion." If the ontologically threatened person feels the self as a vacuum, as empty, then he or she perceives a danger that reality or the world may impinge, rush in to fill that vacuum and overwhelm the self. Laing describes implosion as "the experience of the world as liable at any moment to crash in and obliterate all identity as a gas will rush in and obliterate a vacuum."[17] Both Septimus and Clarissa share an extreme sensitivity to their physical surroundings, which can sometimes become so exciting as to threaten implosion. Woolf describes Septimus's experiences as "this gradual drawing together of everything to one centre before his eyes, as if some horror

had come almost to the surface and was about to burst
into flames" (21). The perception of physical beauty is
often a terrifying experience to Septimus because it
might somehow overwhelm him, drive him more deeply
into madness:

> Happily Rezia put her hand with a tremendous weight
> on his knee so that he was weighted down, transfixed, or
> the excitement of the elm trees rising and falling, rising
> and falling with all their leaves alight and the colour
> thinning and thickening from blue to the green of a
> hollow wave, like plumes on horses' heads, feathers on
> ladies', so proudly they rose and fell, so superbly, would
> have sent him mad. But he would not go mad. He would
> shut his eyes; he would see no more (32).

Clarissa shares Septimus's sensitivity to beauty, as do
all Woolf's feminine characters. Mrs. Ramsay in *To the
Lighthouse*, for example, sees and experiences flowers,
flying rooks, the sea, in a way of which Mr. Ramsay is
incapable. Clarissa's experiences, like Mrs. Ramsay's, are
exciting and revelatory, but they are less intense than
those of Septimus. The sense of implosion, so familiar to
Septimus, is certainly represented in the following
description, although to Clarissa the experience is
momentary, a flash or an epiphany rendered sexually,
an insight into the nature of androgyny which holds no
terror:

> ... yet she could not resist sometimes yielding to the
> charm of a woman, not a girl, of a woman confessing, as
> to her they often did, some scrape, some folly. And wheth-
> er it was pity, or their beauty, or that she was older, or
> some accident—like a faint scent, or a violin next door
> (so strange is the power of sounds at certain moments),
> she did undoubtedly then feel what men felt. Only for a
> moment; but it was enough. It was a sudden revelation, a
> tinge like a blush which one tried to check and then, as it
> spread, one yielded to its expansion, and the world came
> closer, swollen with some astonishing significance, some
> pressure of rapture, which split its thin skin and gushed

and poured with an extraordinary alleviation over the
cracks and sores! Then, for that moment, she had seen
an illumination; a match burning in a crocus; an inner
meaning almost expressed. But the close withdrew; the
hard softened. It was over—the moment (46–47).

Clarissa's revelatory moments are, elusively, only moments, their "inner meaning *almost* expressed," but
not completely. During these brief experiences, however, time itself may be said to be nonexistent for
Clarissa. Morris Beja, in *Epiphany in the Modern Novel*,
writes that during Woolf's many renderings of
epiphanies

> her characters feel that they are in some sort of timeless
> state—that time does not exist, or that it has been sus-
> pended, or that they have escaped it and are outside of
> it. . . . The sense of timelessness would in fact be very
> much like that of living in eternity, or in a world in which
> all time is contemporaneous.[18]

Finally, however, like that of all "sane" people, Clarissa's
escape from time is only temporary. She is ultimately a
victim of a masculine society's creation, real or objective
time, as, throughout the novel, she heeds the ringing of
Big Ben—itself a phallic image—prepares for her party
to be held that evening, and attempts to deal with her
fear of death.

What is only a momentary experience for Clarissa is,
in essence, an eternity for Septimus. His psychosis involves the suspension of objective time; rather he lives
continually in totally subjective time. Like Laing's patients described in *The Politics of Experience*, Septimus
experiences what Laing calls "eonic time" as opposed to
"mundane time":[19] Septimus is free of the limitations
imposed by objective time and thus more open to subjective or revelatory experiences, the consciousness of
the inner self. For Septimus, Woolf writes, "the word
'time' split its husk; poured its riches over him" (105).

Woolf sees such acute subjectivity as painful to endure, but as essentially creative rather than destructive. Mad people *know* things, Woolf intimates, which nominally sane people cannot know; they grapple with monsters of the mind that sane people suppress. Laing goes even further in stating that psychosis can itself be a source of art. In *The Politics of Experience*, he quotes Jean Cocteau: "The creative breath comes from 'a zone of man where man cannot descend, even if Virgil were to lead him, for Virgil would not go down there.'"[20] The descent into madness, says Laing, is akin to a mythical journey from which one can return with a special knowledge and ability:

> From the point of view of a man alienated from its source, creation arises from despair and ends in failure. But such a man has not trodden the path to the end of time, the end of space, the end of darkness, and the end of light. He does not know that where it all ends, there it all begins.[21]

Only when one loses what Laing calls "the Alpha and Omega" can one really begin to write, and then, says Laing, "there is no end to it, words, words, words."[22]

We can also speculate that perhaps Woolf's own periodic mental illness sometimes provided the impetus for her writing, in spite of the fact that the process of writing itself was often agonizing for her. About the composition of *Mrs. Dalloway*, she writes in her diary: "The mad part tries me so much, makes my mind squirt so badly that I can hardly face spending the next weeks at it."[23]

Certainly, Septimus's madness requires that he both talk and write to exhaustion. He prepares voluminous notes addressed to humanity. He identifies himself with Dante, being on a similar journey through the hell of his own mind, and with Shakespeare, with whom, Woolf tells us, Septimus had associated England itself before the war. In his ecstatic apprehension of nature, Septimus is the poet in possession of the meaning of beauty and truth:

> Long streamers of sunlight fawned at his feet. The trees waved, brandished. We welcome, the world seemed to say; we accept; we create. Beauty, the world seemed to say.... To watch a leaf quivering in the rush of air was an exquisite joy ... and the sun spotting now this leaf, now that, in mockery, dazzling it with soft gold in pure good temper; and now and again some chime ... tinkling divinely on the grass stalks—all of this, calm and reasonable as it was, made out of ordinary things as it was, was the truth now; beauty, that was the truth now. Beauty was everywhere. (104–5)

Clarissa, although to a lesser extent, shares this creative force. Her home, with its calm and dignified atmosphere of efficient perfection, all her creation, takes on a religious significance:

> She felt like a nun who has left the world and feels fold round her the familiar veils and the response to old devotions.... It was her life, and, bending her head over the hall table, she bowed beneath the influence, felt blessed and purified (42).

Clarissa's parties, artistic creations in their own right in their combining or unifying of people, are "an offering" (185), becoming associated with a kind of Eastern religious theory of transcendent unity:

> Clarissa had a theory in those days.... It was to explain the feeling they had of dissatisfaction; not knowing people; not being known. For how could they know each other? You met every day; then not for six months, or years. It was unsatisfactory, they agreed, how little one knew people. But she said, sitting on the bus going up Shaftesbury Avenue, she felt herself everywhere; not "here, here, here"; and she tapped the back of the seat; but everywhere. She waved her hand, going up Shaftesbury Avenue. She was all that. So that to know her, or any one, one must seek out the people who completed

them; even the places. Odd affinities she had with
people she had never spoken to, some woman in the
street, some man behind a counter—even trees or barns.
It ended in a transcendental theory which, with her horror of death, allowed her to believe, or say that she believed (for all her scepticism), that since our apparitions,
the part of us which appears, are so momentary compared with the other, the unseen part of us, which
spreads wide, the unseen might survive, be recovered
somehow attached to this person or that, or even haunt-
ing certain places after death . . . perhaps—perhaps
(231–32).

Thus Clarissa, like Jane Eyre although on a more conscious level, rejects the traditional, patriarchal religion
for some more universalized yet subjective concept. It is
difficult, however, to see Clarissa, as does Jean O. Love
in *Worlds in Consciousness*, as *herself* a unity, a kind of
Eastern goddess, "a Brahma-like or Mana-like diety."[24]
Rather, she shares with many of Woolf's other female
and feminine characters what Beja refers to as "a vaguely
'religious' quality."[25]

Clarissa, then, being essentially "sane," apprehends
the mystical only through her experiencing of the
momentary epiphany. Septimus, on the other hand, to
both his terror and joy, lives in a kind of constant
epiphany. The validly mystical experience, Woolf implies, is finally linked to the insane experience.

James Naremore, in *The World Without a Self*, sees
Woolf's epiphanies as "a sacrifice of the ego," connected
with a loss of self in death. Naremore, in fact, describes
Woolf's entire literary style involving the effacement of
the author as indicative of her own death wish.[26] It is
also possible, however, that Woolf does not see the mystical experience, insanity, or even death as a loss of self.
Through his very alienation from the more general illness of society, Septimus is open to an illumination, a
supraconsciousness, which is at least partly a recognition

of the self rather than its loss. He dies, "holding his treasure" (281), while others spend their lives "feeling the impossibility of reaching the centre which, mystically, evaded them" (281).

It is Septimus's visions which provide him with the content of the messages he scribbles so furiously and directs to humanity:

> Men must not cut down trees. There is a God. (He noted such revelations on the backs of envelopes.) Change the world. No one kills from hatred. Make it known (he wrote it down) (35).

Septimus becomes, in his own mind at least, a messiah burdened with the necessity to free humankind from its suffering and delusion. He is the vegetation god in his association with trees, "the leaves being connected by millions of fibres with his own body" (32), and with flowers, which "grew through his flesh" (103). He is the prophet

> raising his hand like some colossal figure who has lamented the fate of man for ages in the desert alone with his hands pressed to his forehead, furrows of despair on his cheeks . . . the giant mourner. . . .
> The millions lamented; for ages they had sorrowed. He would turn round, he would tell them in a few moments, only a few moments more, of this relief, of this joy, of this astonishing revelation—(105–6).

He is T. S. Eliot's drowned sailor, marooned on a rock: "I went under the sea. I have been dead, and yet am now alive" (104). Finally, Septimus is Christ the scapegoat:

> . . . the voice which now communicated with him who was the greatest of mankind, Septimus, lately taken from life to death, the Lord who had come to renew society, who lay like a coverlet, a snow blanket smitten only by the sun, for ever unwasted, suffering for ever, the scapegoat, the eternal sufferer. . . . (37)

Aaron Fleishman, in *Virginia Woolf: A Critical Reading*, writes of Septimus: "The role of Christ figure or lamb of God comes to him not merely out of religious hysteria or personal megalomania, but from his sense of himself as a sacrificial object who affirms the collective existence by separating or sacrificing himself."[27] Septimus's suicide is thus not the mere escape which Sir William Bradshaw thinks it to be, but rather is almost lovingly conceived as an act of martyrdom. Septimus does not want to die, but society demands his sacrifice. "The whole world was clamouring: Kill yourself, kill yourself, for our sakes" (140). As he sits on the window sill, contemplating the jump to the pavement below, Septimus finally capitulates: "I'll give it you!" (226), he says—and jumps.

Laing might well interpret Septimus's suicide as embued with religious significance. Laing writes in *The Politics of Experience* that "there are sudden, apparently inexplicable suicides that must be understood as the dawn of a hope so horrible and harrowing that it is unendurable."[28] For Woolf, unlike Septimus, suicide cannot accomplish the renewal of mankind, but she does endow Septimus's death with symbolic significance: it serves to effect the spiritual regeneration of Clarissa. On being told of Septimus's suicide at her party, Clarissa vicariously dies as well:

> Always her body went through it first, when she was told, suddenly, of an accident; her dress flamed, her body burnt. He had thrown himself from a window. Up had flashed the ground, through him, blundering, bruising, went the rusty spikes. There he lay with a thud, thud, thud in his brain, and then a suffocation of blackness (280).

Clarissa's symbolic death, then, allows her to reaffirm her life. "She felt somehow very like him—the young man who had killed himself. She felt glad that he had done it, thrown it away.... He made her feel the beauty; made her feel the fun" (283-4). Clarissa's desire for unity, *not* at the expense of self, is achieved: "There was an embrace in death" (281). Certainly it is a living, vital, renewed Clarissa who returns to her party, capable of generating in Peter Walsh a "terror," an "ecstasy," an "extraordinary excitement." "It is Clarissa, he said. For there she was" (296).

It is also interesting to note that Septimus serves as a scapegoat for Clarissa on a more literal level as well. According to Woolf's introduction to *Mrs. Dalloway*, which appears in the Modern Library edition, the crea- tion of Septimus was an afterthought; Clarissa herself was originally to have died at the novel's conclusion.

Septimus's death, I think, cannot be seen in the same light as Bertha Mason's death in *Jane Eyre*, though both characters are scapegoats. Harvena Richter, in *The In- ward Voyage*, might better be analyzing Brontë's use of the doppelgänger than Woolf's when she maintains that Septimus represents "the irrational, uncontrolled un- conscious," the bad self, as opposed to Clarissa's "con- trolled, rational conscious."[29] First, it would be unflat- tering to Clarissa, in Woolf's terms, to see her as so very rational, a quality better associated with such characters as Mr. Ramsay in *To the Lighthouse* or even with Sir William Bradshaw, characters who cling to logic in an illogical world, who insist on "proportion" when no such proportion is possible.

Septimus, then, is in a real sense Clarissa's better self. The agony of madness and the loss of life are a terrible price, but Septimus, more than Clarissa, has achieved a sense of self, an integrity, in the face of those who would rob him of such assets. There is nobility in his defiance of the William Bradshaws who insisted that "life was good" (153). Septimus also knew that "life was good" (226), as he indicates just before he jumps to his death—but not on Bradshaw's terms. Therefore, he has "thrown it away" (282). "Death was defiance" (280). Thus what Brontë only dares to hint in her association of Bertha Mason and the crucified Christ, Woolf, like Lessing and Atwood to follow, and like Laing, has affirmed: the psychotic personality is apotheosized.

Laing, like Woolf, rebels against society's views and treatment of what he sees as an almost sacred individual. If, as Laing perceives it, psychosis is a voyage into inner time and space, the result of which is the emergence of an at least quasi-religious figure, if not a saint, then the physician who attends that journey and watches over the traveller ought to assume a religious role as well. He must become what Laing calls "the true physician priest." Laing does not label himself a psychiatrist, but rather "a specialist, God help me, in inner time and space."[30] Instead of the "degradation ceremonial" of the psychiatric examination, Laing suggests, there should be substituted a kind of initiation ceremony to guide the voyager through his journey and to help him back again.[31] Perhaps, Laing says, "we will learn to accord to so-called schizophrenics who have come back to us, perhaps after years, no less respect than the often no less lost explorers of the Renaissance."[32] The figure of Septimus as scapegoat, as victim of society's own illnesses called war, oppression, and insensitivity, serves well to illustrate the real meaning of the word "schizophrenia," which, Laing says, literally translates "brokenhearted." And, writes Laing, "even broken hearts have been known to mend if we have the heart to let them."[33]

Woolf, too, opposes the authority of professional power. For her, it is a political and philosophical atrocity that Sir William Bradshaw has the right to "shut people up" and to violate the sacred area of the mind. As E. M. Forster writes of Woolf, "she was always civilized and sane on the subject of madness."[34] Woolf, like Laing, indicates that insanity, after all, may be the only escape from society's own state of schizophrenia called normality. Sanity and insanity, then, are designated as polarities only by a society, largely masculine in its assumption of power, whose own "sanity" depends on such distinctions.

3

"A Rehearsal for Madness": *Hysteria as Sanity in* The Four-Gated City

The invisible woman in the asylum corridor
sees others quite clearly,
including the doctor who patiently tells her
she isn't invisible,
and pities the doctor, who must be mad
to stand there in the asylum corridor,
talking and gesturing
to nothing at all.

The invisible woman has great compassion.
So, after a while, she pulls on her body
like a rumpled glove, and switches on her voice
to comfort the elated doctor with words.
Better to suffer this prominence
than for the poor young doctor to learn
he himself is insane.
Only the strong can know that.

Robin Morgan,
"The Invisible Woman"

But the most frightening thing about them was this: that they walked and moved and went about their lives in a condition of sleepwalking: they were not aware of themselves, of other people, of what went on around them ... they stood with the masses of pelt hanging around their faces, and the slits in their faces stretched in the sounds they made to communicate, or as they emitted a series of loud noisy breaths which was a way of indicating surprise or a need to release tension ... each seemed locked in an invisible cage which prevented him from experiencing his fellow's thoughts, or lives, or needs. They were essentially isolated, shut in, enclosed inside their hideously defective bodies, behind their dreaming drugged eyes, above all, inside a net of wants and needs that made it impossible for them to think of anything else.[1]

These lines do not depict, as might be expected, the insanity of a grotesque and subhuman Bertha Mason; nor do they describe that troop of pathetic lunatics being marched through the streets of London to the horror of Septimus Warren Smith in *Mrs. Dalloway*. Rather, this is a description of the "normal" members of society, the majority of humanity, as perceived by what can be termed the "psychotic" mind, that which for Doris Lessing in *The Four-Gated City* is the only mind sufficiently sensitive to apprehend reality objectively.

Lessing's rendition of this reality, apparent in the en-

67

tire *Children of Violence* series of which *The Four-Gated City* is the culmination, is a world that Brontë, for all her sense of evil, could hardly have conceived; it is the world of Clarissa Dalloway's worst apprehensions now fully and socially realized. Truth, for Lessing, is first presented in *The Four-Gated City* as that nightmare vision of post-World-War-II London seen by the self-proclaimed hysteric, Martha Quest Hesse. "Martha the traveller" (80) homelessly walks the streets, finding her way across great pits left by exploded bombs and through crowds of depressed and poverty-stricken humanity. The entire world seems to her to be numb, blinded. Martha alone perceives her own plight and the plight of others as she observes, "there's something wrong with me that I do see what's going on as ugly, as if I were the only person awake and everyone else is in a kind of bad dream, but they couldn't see that they were" (68). Society seems oblivious to the fact that it is oppressed, that war is an unbelievable atrocity, that there are "a number of events, or processes, in this or that part of the world, whose common quality was horror—and a senseless horror . . . this barbarism, this savagery was simply not possible" (198).

Martha is later in the novel to meet a few people, like her employer and lover, the author Mark Coldridge, who are also aware that political and philosophical oppression—which includes racism, sexism, any sort of "ism" which manipulates power—is responsible for unspeakable acts perpetrated on human beings and on the physical world in which they live. But Mark must discipline himself to learn what Martha, in her acute state of perception, already feels; he must constantly remind himself of reality by filling an entire room with maps and headlines, the physical evidence of truth:

> On the walls multiplied the charts of the death factories, the poison factories, the factories that made instruments

for the control of the mind: the maps of Hunger, Pov-
erty, Riot and the rest; the atlases of poisoned air and
poisoned earth and the places where bombs had been
exploded under the sea, where atomic waste was sunk
into the sea, where ships discharged filthy oil into the
sea, where inland waters were dead or dying (379).

Thus there is a kind of reverse progression from
Brontë to Lessing: the individual "he" as enemy in
Brontë's novel and the more universalized "He" as the
quality of negative masculinity in Woolf's, become, in
The Four-Gated City, an even more ominous because less
easily identifiable "They," responsible for the fact that
the entire world is war-torn, physically and morally dis-
eased, and, ultimately, by the end of the novel, to destroy itself through germ warfare.

Lessing, like Woolf, sees "normality" or the adjustment to such a state of affairs as itself a form of madness. A similar definition of normality is professed by R.
D. Laing, whom Lessing has referred to as "a peg," a
"key authority figure."[2] In *The Politics of Experience*
Laing writes that "only by the most outrageous violation
of ourselves have we achieved our capacity to live in
relative adjustment to a civilization apparently driven to
its own destruction."[3]

Martha can specifically identify the particular form of
madness which afflicts all of society as she becomes increasingly aware that the state of normality is one of
schizophrenia, of alienation; it is "a condition of dis-
parateness," the separate parts of the mind "working
individually, by themselves, not joining" (61). Human
beings by definition are mad, according to Lessing, because the human brain itself is "a machine which works
in division; it is composed of parts which function in
compartments locked off from each other: or 'your
right hand does not know what your left hand is doing'"
(496). In her critical biography of Lessing, Dorothy

Brewster quotes Lessing's childhood memory of her father, sitting in a chair, looking out over the vast Rhodesian landscape and periodically shaking his fist at the sky and shouting, "Mad—everyone—everywhere!"[4]

Laing's description of schizophrenia corresponds to Lessing's: he sees it as, first, an alienation from the self, which leads to an alienation from other people as well, and this condition, Laing states, is virtually universal. We live, he writes, "in an age of darkness."[5] Lessing too sees the world as "a country where people could not communicate across the dark that separates them" (79). Communication of any kind, verbal or sexual, is almost an impossibility in Lessing's novel, the whole of which might be seen to serve as a negative answer, at least for this time, to Laing's terrifying question: "Is love possible?"[6]

Lessing describes sex, for example, as an act in which people temporarily "plug into" each other (471). "Passion," that term which has such reality and meaning in the works of Brontë and Woolf, which so permeates the consciousness and inspires such dread in the earlier works, hardly exists as a concept in Lessing's world. "We don't understand the first thing about what goes on," she writes, "not the first thing. 'Make love,' 'Make sex,' 'orgasms,' 'climaxes'—it was all nonsense, words, sounds, invented by half-animals who understood nothing at all" (470).

The single scene in *The Four-Gated City* which might be considered at all erotic is that enacted between Martha and Jack, who is a kind of sexual athlete and who, later in the novel, will completely pervert sexual relationships by seducing women into prostitution. Even in this scene, however, sex cannot really be considered a form of communication, the participants being locked into their own purely subjective experiences, meeting needs that are solely individual, getting from each other a compensation for personal traumas of the past. Jack has suffered terribly in the war, and now one woman serves as well as another to feed his terrible hunger for experience, for life.

Martha and Mark Coldridge also have a sexual relationship, primarily because it is convenient and serves as an outlet for the extreme pressures each is under. Mark can go from a series of premarital relationships to his wife Lynda to Martha to the brainless Rita—and it is all the same. No confrontation, no announcement precedes the end of his affair with Martha, who calmly accepts her rejection and goes on to other nondescript relationships. "When it's a question of survival, sex the uncontrollable can be controlled. And therefore had Martha joined that band of women who have affairs because men have ceased to be explorations into unknown possibilities" (287).

Love is only a word; the reality is subjective need, and sex itself, says Martha, is a force "as impersonal as thunder or lightning" (470). One is reminded of that African scene in Lessing's *The Golden Notebook* in which millions upon millions of copulating grasshoppers, indifferent as to their partners, frenziedly and blindly fulfill the dictates of some mad god called nature.

Martha also sees marriage as a part of this universal mockery. "The truth was, she feared marriage, looking at it from outside now, unable to believe that she had ever been in it. What an institution! What an absurd arrangement. . . ." (286) Marriage is such an appalling situation for Martha because she sees it, like all other human relationships, as based on subjective need, selfish concerns, the use of one person by another. Women, as well as men, self-centeredly seek some impossible fulfillment. Martha recognizes and rejects this tendency toward subjectivity in herself as well as in others:

> But to herself she was able to say precisely what she feared. It was the rebirth of the woman in love. If one is with a man, "in love," or in the condition of loving, then

> there comes to life that hungry, never-to-be-fed, never-at-peace woman who needs and wants and must have. That creature had come into existence with Mark. She would come into existence again. For the unappeasable hungers and the cravings are part, not of the casual affair, or of friendly sex, but of marriage and the "serious" love. God forbid.
>
> ... when a woman has reached that point when she allies part of herself with the man who will feed that poor craving bitch in every woman, then enough, it's time to move on (286–87).

In her short story "To Room Nineteen," Lessing suggests that even a "perfect" marriage, based supposedly on intelligence and mutual respect, can become merely an animal-like struggle to meet subjective desires. In this case the husband wins, and the wife, *her* needs completely unmet, kills herself.

Like Woolf, Lessing sees the horrors of the public world reflected in the private world of marriage. Society in Lessing's work is no more capable of permitting the reality of Martha's dream of "the Golden Age" in which a man, woman, and beautiful children join hands and walk "in a high place under a blue sky" (59) than it is of attaining the utopia of the ordered and peaceful "four-gated city."

Perhaps, however, it is the very depersonalization of sex which, for Lessing, contributes to the possibility of psychological survival in a mad world. As chastity and inaccessibility operate to protect the self from annihilation in the works of Brontë and Woolf, so Lessing sees numerous sexual experiences as precluding the possibility of total engulfment in the one. Janet Sydney Kaplan, in her article "The Limits of Consciousness in the Novels of Doris Lessing," states that Martha fears the loss of ego in the sexual relationship.[7] However, if the self is not extended and made vulnerable in sex, if "the craving bitch" is suppressed, if sex is kept impersonal, "casual," "friendly" (impossible concepts for either Woolf or Brontë), then the self is protected as efficiently as if there were no sex act at all. Such a character as Sally-Sarah, in loving a husband who is totally immersed in such abstractions as science and communism at the expense of personal relationships, is tragic because she does extend the self. Like the wife in "To Room Nineteen," Sally-Sarah ends by committing suicide. A woman who survives (at least physically), on the other hand, is the promiscuous Jill, who most often has no notion of the identity of the father of the current child she is bearing.

If the term "love" must be qualified out of existence in Lessing's world, so must words like "hate," which emotion becomes merely another aspect of the normal state of alienation, providing none of the gratification or purgative function so necessary in the novels of Brontë and Woolf. Jack explains and Martha concurs:

> "You say all your life *I hate, I love*. But then you discover hatred is a sort of wavelength you can tune into. After all, it's always there, hatred is simply part of the world, like one of the colours of the rainbow. You can go into it, as if it were a *place*" (57).

"Love" and "hate" then, because each implies an object, have a limited meaning. They are words empty of significance. All human feeling can in essence be reduced to subjectivity, which Lessing sees as synonomous with alienation. However, as Lessing indicates in her introduction to *The Golden Notebook*, to recognize this subjectivity as inherent in the human condition, as universal, is ultimately to break through the barriers which it erects:

> The way to deal with the problem of "subjectivity," that shocking business of being preoccupied with the tiny individual who is at the same time caught up in such an explosion of terrible and marvelous possibilities, is to see

> him as a microcosm and in this way to break through the
> personal, the subjective, making the personal general, as
> indeed life always does, transforming a private ex-
> perience . . . into something much larger: growing up is
> after all only the understanding that one's unique and
> incredible experience is what everyone shares.[8]

In the author's notes appended to *The Four-Gated City*,
Lessing describes her novel as a bildungsroman.
Martha, then, "grows up" because she comes to see her
own schizophrenia and subjectivity projected into the
world at large. Only through the recognition of one's
own madness as a reflection of the world's madness can
a higher state of sanity be achieved. Conscious madness,
as opposed to the world's *un*conscious madness, is the
way to truth itself for Lessing:

> Perhaps it was because if society is so organized, or
> rather has so grown, that it will not admit what one
> knows to be true, will not admit it, that is, except as it
> comes out perverted, through madness, then it is
> through madness and its variants it must be sought after
> (357).

"Madness" and "sanity" thus become, like "love" and
"hate," meaningless terms, their significance merely a
matter of perception: "Better mad, if the price for not
being mad is to be a lump of lethargy that will use any
kind of strategem so as to remain a lump, remain non-
perceptive and heavy" (484).

Laing, particularly in his later works, similarly maintains that there is a positive function for what society
terms madness; that it is not "what we need to be cured
of, but that it is itself a natural way of healing our own
appalling state of alienation called normality."[9] Normality, for Laing and for Lessing, is the negative and truly
insane state, because it implies the clinging to uncertain
certainties and the dependence on a reality that is, in
fact, unreal. To go mad in a positive sense is to give up

all certainty, according to Laing and Lessing, to lose the distinction between the real and the not-real, between the self and the not-self. Laing and Lessing both indicate that the result of going mad in this sense may well be the emergence of a state of mind far saner than that understood by the normal world. Similarly, Woolf's Septimus in *Mrs. Dalloway* is a "saner" person than his evil physician.

Martha Quest is perhaps named for her search for this superior sanity, which she begins through a virtually self-conscious and planned inducement of hysteria, a state she describes as "a rehearsal":

> When you get to a new place in yourself, when you are going to break into something new, then it sometimes is presented to you like that: giggling and tears and hysteria. It's a thing you'll understand properly one day— being tested out. First you have to accept them like that, silly and giggly.... (69)

Hysteria thus is a rehearsal for the madness which will lead to enlightenment:

> Yes—hysteria. This country, the country or sea, of sound, the wavelength where the voices babble and rage and sing and laugh, and music and war sounds and the bird song and every conceivable sound go together, was approached, at least for her, or at least at this time, through hysteria. Very well then, she would be hysterical (491).

Martha also experiments with the possibilities of surrendering identity, of obscuring the distinction between the self and the not-self, not through a loss of self in the sexual experience, as Kaplan suggests,[10] but in the more easily controlled area of her own mind. She recognizes that she has always, since childhood, maintained "as an act of survival" a second personality, a false aspect of the self, a "parody" called "Matty" (5). Now she can clinically observe her own schizophrenia: she can "call strange identities into being with a switch of clothes or a change of voice—until one felt like an empty space without boundaries and it did not matter what name one gave a stranger who asked: What is your name? Who are you?" (17)

Name and identity, so inextricably connected in the works of both Brontë and Woolf that the loss of one in marriage threatens the loss of the other, are also important links in Lessing's novel. Sally-Sarah, for example, is really just "Sarah," but her husband's family, seeking to disguise her Jewish background, renames her "Sally." Perhaps her inability to herself control whether she is Sally or Sarah is another contributing factor to her suicide. For Martha, however, this connection between name and identity is part of the rehearsal, a crucial factor in the experiment of surrendering identity, so serious that she refers to it as her "work":

> As for "Hesse," it was a name acquired like a bracelet from a man who had it in his possession to be given to a woman in front of lawyers at the time of the signing of the marriage contract. But who then was she, behind the banalities of the day? . . . But really, there she was: *she* was, nothing to do with Martha, or any other name she might have attached to her. . . . (36)

Thus madness and the loss of identity, those states which Jane Eyre and Clarissa Dalloway struggle to avoid, Martha actively seeks to confront. She realizes that she can move almost at will from "inside the empty space of self" into "ordinary living" in which the self "seemed a very far country" (8). She experiments in this way because, paradoxically, only through the loss of self is it possible to find the self:

> Sometimes she felt like a person who wakes up in a strange city, not knowing who he, she, is. There she sat, herself. Her name was Martha, a convenient label to attach to her sense of herself. Sometimes she got up and

> looked into the mirror, in an urgency of need to see a
> reflection of that presence called, for no particular rea-
> son, Martha. She had dark eyes. She smiled, or frowned.
> Once, bringing to the mirror a mood of seething anxiety,
> she saw a dishevelled panic-struck creature biting its
> nails. She watched this creature, who was in an agony of
> fear. Who watched? (215)

Martha's question is not fully answered until she meets
Lynda Coldridge, who will, by example, guide Martha
from hysteria into the insane experience where the true
identity of the self is to be discovered. Perhaps it is in
much the same way that Woolf perceives Septimus to
have kept or even to have gained his "treasure" of the
self in madness. Lynda also echoes Septimus's claim to
superior knowledge, expressed in the urgent message
he directs to humanity. Throughout Lessing's novel
Lynda repeats: "I know things." Part of what she knows
is that all people are really at least two people: "Sometimes you are more the one that watches, and sometimes
that one gets far off and you are more the one that is
watched" (216). Martha too becomes aware of "the some-
body in you who always watches what goes on, who is
always apart" (228).

As Brontë's Bertha can be seen as Jane Eyre's mad,
bad self, so Lynda can be seen as Martha's mad, good
self. She serves as both guide and doppelgänger.
Martha feels this identification even before she meets
Lynda.

> ... she had not met Lynda, save through improbably
> beautiful photographs, but she knew her, oh yes, very well,
> though she and Martha were not alike, and could not be,
> since Martha was not "ill" and in the hands of the doc-
> tors. But for a large variety of reasons, Lynda Coldridge,
> who was in a very expensive mental hospital because she
> could not stand being Mark's wife, and Francis's mother,
> came too close to Martha. Which was why Martha had to
> leave this house and soon (109).

Martha cannot, however, simply leave, being held, at least partly, by this mysterious affinity with the insane Lynda. Because Lynda cannot "stand being Mark's wife" and refuses sexual intimacy with him, Martha assumes Lynda's role and becomes Mark's surrogate wife, sleeping with him, caring for his son and nephew, managing his house, providing him with ideas for his novel and plays. When Mark turns his attentions from Martha, she moves into Lynda's apartment in the basement, where their relationship as doubles is further emphasized, where Martha comes to realize that she is "in love" with Lynda as "with a part of herself she had never even been introduced to—even caught a glimpse of" (351). As Martha enters Lynda's mad world, both physically and emotionally, she sometimes wonders where she ends and where Lynda begins. In describing the chaos of sound which is a part of her insane experience, Martha asks, "Is it in Lynda's head or in mine?" (473) At that point in their shared experience at which the world seems the furthest removed, Lynda and Martha together perform a kind of ritual, like a communion, Lynda kneeling on the floor and, animal-like, lapping milk from a broken saucer, and Martha drinking "symbolically" from the same saucer (465).

The character of Lynda could well be seen as a parody of Brontë's Bertha, not only in her function as doppelgänger, but in other areas as well. Both Lynda and Bertha are women of great former beauty, now ravaged by madness. Bertha, however, is bloated and gigantized, while Lynda has shrunk into "a creature all bone, with yellowish-smelling flesh, with great anxious globes of water tinted blue stuck in its face" (492). Bertha is dark; Lynda is pale blonde. Bertha's laughter is maniacal and blood-chilling; Lynda's uncontrollable "giggling" is equally maniacal, but sad rather than grotesque. Bertha is violent against selected others; Lynda is only violent

against herself as she deprives her emaciated body of
food and repeatedly pounds her head against the walls.
Lynda lives in the basement, a location perhaps more
appropriate as a symbolic hell than the attic room in
which Bertha is confined. Lynda gropes at the walls of
her room, not seeking escape as Bertha does, but rather
exploring them as symbolically representing the walls of
her own mind. Bertha represents passion and sexual
excess; Lynda is chaste, the imaginary Guru of the vision she shares with Martha having told her that "the
Great Mother" has chosen her as "one of her daughters
who had been freed of the tyrannies of the flesh—lust,
he said" (475). Bertha enters Jane's room to tear the
wedding veil, her motive, Rochester suggests, being the
desecration of the memory of her own bridal days.
Lynda enters her husband's room on a similar errand,
the destruction of her own beautiful photograph. Bertha paces and creeps in her confinement; Lynda shares
a similar need for constant and seemingly motiveless
movement. In a scene strikingly similar to those depicted in yet another story about a mad woman, Charlotte Perkins Gilman's "The Yellow Wallpaper," Lynda
arranges her allotted space:

> . . . around the walls there was a clear space or runway, as
> if there were a second invisible wall against which a table,
> chairs, bookcases, were arranged, a yard or so inside the
> visible wall. And again, all around the walls to the height
> of about five feet the paper had an irregularly smudged
> and rusty look, which turned out to be the bloodstains
> from Lynda's bitten finger ends (461–62).

The most important similarity between Brontë's and
Lessing's mad characters is their common function as
scapegoat, a role which Lynda consciously recognizes as
her own (493). Because she is powerless and female, she,
like Bertha, suffers for the sins of both father and husband. Lynda's father, frustrated in his attempts at re-

marriage by his daughter's strange behavior toward his intended wife, "handed her bound and helpless to the doctors, where she had struggled and fought and been bludgeoned into silence by drugs and injections, held down by nurses and dragged screaming to have electric shocks" (495). Mark, in contrast to Lynda's father and to Brontë's Rochester, appears patient and devoted, but in reality, one suspects, he is enjoying his role as long-suffering martyr; he has played it before with other "neurotic" problem women and will assume it again with Martha and others as well. Perhaps Lynda is perceptive rather than ungrateful when she echoes Jane Eyre's cry to St. John Rivers, "Leave me alone.... You're killing me" (181). Mark, after all, is a part of normal society, and therefore ill equipped to understand Lynda. He, like her father, eventually turns her over "into the hands of the doctors."

As Marion Vlastos states in the article "Doris Lessing and R. D. Laing: Psychopolitics and Prophecy," Lynda is also a scapegoat in the sense that she is "a victim of society's mistrust of the strange and the acutely sensitive."[11] The same description applies to Woolf's Septimus. Too, Lessing's ironically named Dr. Lamb, Lynda's psychiatrist, is a symbolic representation of that mistrusting society, in much the same way that Sir William Bradshaw represents the negative elements in Woolf's world. Like Bradshaw, Dr. Lamb is emotionless, courteous, sexless, and professional. He echoes Bradshaw's very words as he promises Martha that after her analysis she will see her problems "in proportion" (235). He appears to Martha "like a character in a play who wore a mask which said, 'I am Wisdom'" (223). Lynda screams that he is the devil, and Martha perceives with horror that he is the incarnation of power itself:

> There was nobody, ever, who could approach Dr. Lamb without a certain kind of tremor. When he spoke to law courts, or advised policemen, or sat in judgement

about this sick person or that: when a mortally confused human being sat before him, what Dr. Lamb said was the truth.... Dr. Lamb, whether benign, cruel, a secret lover of power, or a man gifted with insight, was always in a position of strength. Because it was he who knew—society had said he did—everything that could be known about the human soul....

The central fact here was that nobody approched Dr. Lamb unless he had to. In approaching Dr. Lamb one approached power. It was hard to think of a power like it, in its inclusiveness, its arbitrariness, its freedom to behave as it wished, without checks from other places or powers (305–6).

Sir William Bradshaw humiliates his patients by forcing them to drink milk in bed, but Dr. Lamb's medications are far more potent. Lessing, like Laing and a growing number of other modern psychologists, is opposed to many of the traditional therapeutic treatments, including the use of drugs to simulate normality. Lynda is most pathetic when she has lost control of her illness because of her addiction to and dependence on medications. Both drugs and shock treatments are, to Lessing's mind, no more than torture devices, methods used to punish and control.

Lessing also shares Laing's views regarding the dangers of the traditional analyst-patient relationship. Laing writes:

> Psychotherapy must remain *an obstinate attempt of two people to recover the wholeness of being human through the relationship between them.*
>
> Any technique concerned with the other without the self, with behavior to the exclusion of experience, with the relationship to the neglect of the persons in relation, with the individuals to the exclusion of their relationship, and most of all, with an object-to-be-changed rather than a person-to-be-accepted, simply perpetuates the disease it purports to cure.[12]

Lessing too rejects the idea of the analyst as authority figure and sees it as disastrous when "the patient became dependent on the doctor and was unable to free himself" (583).

Lessing, also like Laing, deplores the existence of mental hospitals, those institutions which, Laing says, imprison the insane person, leaving him or her "bereft of his civil liberties . . . invalidated as a human being."[13] Lessing describes the politics of mental illness:

> Some years before, an act of Parliament had been passed, which had taken bars off windows, unlocked doors, made strait jackets and padded cells things of the past, created hospitals that were civilized. Well, not quite. Because, for this bit of legal well-wishing to work, it needed that a great deal of money should be spent on new buildings, doctors, nurses. This money was not being spent. (It was being spent on war, the central fact of our time which is taken for granted.)
>
> Inside the dozens of mental hospitals scattered up and down the country, built like prisons, were many thousands of people who had been strait-jacketed, forcibly fed, kept in padded cells, beaten (in fact, the central fact, had had their wills broken), and were now derelict, "deteriorated" (308).

Normal people perpetrate such obscenities, not out of gratuitous cruelty, according to Lessing, but out of fear that prevents their recognition of themselves as mad and out of the suspicion that the "insane" person possesses a superior sanity:

> They are so susceptible to flattery that anything may be done with them; provided they are not allowed to suspect their inferiority. For they are so vain that they would certainly kill or imprison or maim any being they suspect of being better endowed than themselves (482).

Thus, Lynda repeatedly warns Martha never to tell "them" what she knows.

Insane women of today, writes Lessing, are like the witches of former centuries, tortured because they have superior capacities. Virginia Woolf, too, frequently makes a connection in her nonfiction works between the witches of history, the wise women, and present-day victims of mental illness. She writes in *A Room of One's Own*:

> Any woman born with a great gift in the sixteenth century would certainly have gone crazed, shot herself, or ended her days in some lonely cottage outside the village, half witch, half wizard, feared and mocked at. For it needs little skill in psychology to be sure that a highly gifted girl who had tried to use her gift for poetry would have been so thwarted and hindered by other people, so tortured and pulled asunder by her own contrary instincts, that she must have lost her health and sanity to a certainty.[14]

Bertha Mason or even Jane Eyre herself with her presentiments, her prophetic dreams, her affinity with both nature and the supernatural, may be more witchlike than Lynda and Martha, yet Lessing's characters, through their mutual experiencing of insanity, do delve into the occult and emerge with what Lessing calls a "new sort of understanding" (357):

> Yet in their own inner experience this was a time of possibility. It was as if doors kept opening in their brains just far enough to admit a new sensation, or a glimmer of something—and though they closed again, something was left behind ... they understood what it meant that "scales should fall from one's eyes"—scales had fallen (356).

"Madness," according to Laing, "need not be all breakdown. It may also be breakthrough, It is potentially liberation and renewal as well as enslavement and existential death."[15]

Certainly, what Martha feels when she comes up from the basement, after many days of sharing an intense and often terrifying experience with Lynda, is what Dante must have felt as he exited from hell, or what Woolf's Septimus experiences in his most ecstatic visions: a sense of resurrection, of rebirth. Each moment, for Martha, becomes an epiphany, a miracle:

> The words kept dropping into the listening space that was Martha's mind. She knew that if a person were to take one word, and listen; or a pebble or a jewel and look at it; the word, the stone, would give up, in the end, its own meaning and the meaning of everything (470).

Laing says that "our social realities are so ugly if seen in the light of exiled truth."[16] Just as Martha has perceived through her hysteria the ugliness of reality and of humanity, so she also deeply experiences, through the "light of exiled truth," the physical beauty of the world. Like Septimus, she can perceive the universe as magnificent. The sky hangs above her "an explosion of golden light" (482), and the world, like her resurrected self, seems new:

> The day was fresh and the world newly painted. She stood on a pavement looking at a sky where soft white clouds were lit with sunlight. She wanted to cry because it was so beautiful. How long since she had looked, but really looked, at the sky, so beautiful even if it was held up by tall buildings? She stood gazing up, up, until her eyes seemed absorbed in the crystalline substance of the sky with its blocks of clouds like snowbanks, she seemed to be streaming out through her eyes into the skies. . . . (478–79)

There are, however, also the nightmare aspects of the insane experience to be dealt with. For Martha, as for Septimus, there is the fear of losing control, the necessity to close one's eyes so that the visions do not become too beautiful, too terrifying. For Lynda and Martha, there is also the "sound barrier" to be got through, a barrage of noise which becomes excruciating and must, eventually, be sorted out and made rational. The "radio" in one's head is tuned simultaneously to a hundred stations, and one must fight to gain control.

Worst of all the mad experiences is the confrontation with what Lessing calls the "self-hater," that evil in the schizophrenic self which balances or sometimes annihilates the good. Lynda, having lost control and having been victimized by drugs and doctors, is never able successfully to combat the "self-hater," but Martha, free of impediments, eventually goes on alone to conquer it.

It is during this particular battle that Martha most clearly recognizes that the self is the microcosm and that it, like the world, is divided between victim and tormentor: Martha herself is both "the ragged bit of refuse (me) pushed into the gas chamber and the uniformed woman (me) who pushed" (510). Woolf's Septimus perhaps experiences a similar confrontation: he feels himself guilty of terrible crimes against humanity while, at the same time, he sees himself as Christ. Lessing's description of Martha's recognition of the "self-hater" is equally paradoxical and equally imbued with religious significance:

> From the moment when Pontius Pilate washed his hands to the time when she, Martha, who was also the Devil, prepared to be bound on the Cross, because of the frightfulness of her crimes, she was as it were whipped through the ritual by the hating scourging tongue of the Devil who was her self, her hating, self-hating self (522).

Recognition of and confrontation with the "self-hater" are, according to Lessing, prerequisites for knowledge of the divided self and the first steps to making it whole.

The state of insanity, then, is divided between the regions of joy and beauty, poetry and religion, and the regions of terror. Normal adult people, Lessing says, never experience these extremes of feeling because they fear any disturbance of complacency. Martha, however, strives to recall and to reattain the sensitivity and perception, the extremes of feeling, which she recalls as a part of childhood:

> The first intimations of this capacity had been in child-
> hood, just before sleep or on awakening: a faint flash of
> colour, a couple of pictures perhaps, or a fragment of
> music, or some words, or her name called in warning or
> reminder: *Remember, remember.* Well, a great many
> people experienced this, but being well-ordered, well-
> trained, docile, obedient people, they heard the doctors
> or the priests say—whatever the current dogma ordered
> and that was that: they were prepared to bury the evi-
> dence of their own senses, they ran away. And like any
> neglected faculty, it fell into disuse, it atrophied (484).

Lessing's romantic idea is that children are thus somehow in touch with something mystical with which adults
have lost contact. Laing, throughout *The Politics of Experience*, maintains a similar notion: "As adults, we have
forgotten most of our childhood, not only its contents
but its flavor; as men of the world, we hardly know of
the existence of the inner world."[17]

Both Martha and Lynda are loved by children and
have a strange ability to communicate with them beyond
what is possible for normal adults. Lynda, during some
of her worst periods in the basement, shuts out the adult
world, but admits her nephew and, later, her son. They
understand her and she them, but because of her pref-
erence for the company of children, the doctors pro-
nounce her behavior regressive.

Although Martha acts as a surrogate mother to Lynda's son, she has, before the novel begins, abandoned
her own daughter. A possible reason for this action is
that her relationship with her own mother has been so
devastatingly disappointing, so guilt-ridden and nonlov-
ing. Yet Martha longs for maternal love. In a state of
depression, dreading the approaching visit of her
mother, Martha weeps "while a small girl wept with her,
Mama, Mama, why are you so cold, so unkind, why did
you never love me?" (221) Martha anticipates this visit in
a state, virtually, of emotional prostration, yet she pro-

vides for Dr. Lamb only the formulaic reasons for her feelings: "My mother was a woman who hated her own sexuality and she hated mine too" (230).

Laing, like Lessing, sees children as irreparably damaged in the mother-child relationship which in present society, he says, is one of violence and devastation:

> Children are not yet fools, but we shall turn them into imbeciles like ourselves with high I.Q.'s if possible.
>
> From the moment of birth, when the Stone Age baby confronts the twentieth-century mother, the baby is subjected to these forces of violence, called love, as its mother and father and their parents and their parents before them, have been. These forces are mainly concerned with destroying most of its potentialities, and on the whole this enterprise is successful. By the time the new human being is fifteen or so, we are left with a being like ourselves, a half-crazed creature more or less adjusted to a mad world.[18]

With Laing's statement in mind, it is perhaps easier to understand Martha's explanation for abandoning her child: "When I left my little girl, Caroline, do you know what I was thinking? I thought, I'm setting you free, I thought, I'm setting you free...." (66)

Martha, like Jane Eyre, is unsuccessful in her search for mother love, but unlike Jane, Martha has a great capacity to assume the maternal role herself, at least with others than her own child. Martha's relationship with Mark, for example, is distinguished by a "protective compassion"; she would like to surround both him and herself with "invisible arms, vast, peaceful, maternal" (468). Martha's feeling for Lynda is less a lesbian-oriented love than a longing to mother. "This unknown person in Martha adored Lynda, worshipped her, wished to wrap her long soft hair around her hands, said, Poor little child, poor little girl, why don't you let me look after you?" (252)

Perhaps disinterested, nonpossessive maternal love is

the only kind of love possible in Lessing's world; it may, in fact, provide at least a relative salvation for all of humanity. Martha's nurturing instincts finally permit her to assume the mother role to hundreds of special children who survive the earth's devastation at the end of the novel. Martha knows that these "freak" children, some anomalies born after the apocalyptic event, are really supranormal, highly sensitive and, like "mad" persons, able to "see" and to "hear" things. They are, possibly, to provide the rebirth of the world; they can, potentially, create a new world, one which might not sink into darkness and schizophrenia, but might remain whole, perceptive, undivided, like that world ruled by the gods and goddesses of Lessing's *Briefing for a Descent into Hell*. Laing, too, sees the world's hope in children:

> Each time a new baby is born there is a possibility of reprieve. Each child is a new being, a potential prophet, a new spiritual prince, a new spark of light precipitated into the outer darkness. Who are we to decide it is hopeless?[19]

Martha herself does not live to see any such hope fulfilled. The Edenic return possible for Jane Eyre and the self-affirmation possible for Clarissa are not probabilities in Lessing's bleaker world. Near the end of the novel, Martha is an old woman alone; however, her hysteria is calmed, her self fully discovered and recognized, if not healed:

> She walked beside the river while the music thudded, feeling herself as a heavy impervious lump that, like a planet doomed always to be dark on one side, had vision in front only, a myopic search-light, blind except for the tiny three-dimensional path open immediately before her eyes in which the outline of a tree, a rose, emerged, then submerged in the dark. She thought, with the dove's voices of her solitude: Where? But *where*. How? Who? No, but *where*, where... Then silence and the

birth of a repetition: *Where?* Here. Here?
  Here, where else, you fool, you poor fool, where else
has it been, ever . . . (559)

Hysteria, after all, is literally a suffering in the womb. In helping to give birth to a potentially better world, Martha is left with at least a knowledge, a vision, which consoles.

4

"After the Failure of Logic": Descent and Return in Surfacing

The country beneath
the earth has a green sun
and the rivers flow backwards;

the trees and rocks are the same
as they are here, but shifted.
Those who live there are always hungry;

from them you can learn
wisdom and great power,
if you can descend and return safely.

. . .

Margaret Atwood,
"Procedures for Underground"

IT IS INEVITABLE for Margaret Atwood's nameless protagonist of *Surfacing* that there should occur a "failure of logic,"[1] for her journey "home" is an exploration of a world beyond logic. Her quest, like that of Jane Eyre, Clarissa Dalloway, and Martha Quest Hesse, is for an identity, a vision of self. She must find that self—not only through the father for whom she searches the Canadian backwoods, but also through the mother for whom she must search in the depths of her own psyche.

Atwood, much like Virginia Woolf, juxtaposes and compares two internal worlds: the world of the male principle, characterized by rationality and logic but often also by cruelty and destruction, and the world of the female principle, which for Atwood implies an existence beyond reason, a realm of primitive nature where there are connections between life and death, suffering and joy, madness and true sanity, where opposites are resolved into wholes. A failure to recognize these connections is a failure to perceive the "female" part of one's self, and this results, for Atwood, in a catastrophic splitting of the self. Like R. D. Laing's patients in *The Divided Self*, alienated from the self and from society,[2] Atwood's protagonist perceives herself as rent, torn asunder:

> I'd allowed myself to be cut in two. Woman sawn apart in
> a wooden crate, wearing a bathing suit, smiling, a trick

93

> done with mirrors, I read it in a comic book; only with
> me there had been an accident and I came apart. The
> other half, the one locked away, was the only one that
> could live; I was the wrong half, detached, terminal. I
> was nothing but a head, or, no, something minor like a
> severed thumb; numb (124–25).

The protagonist has separated her body from her head, divided the parts of her self, and thus committed psychological suicide: "If the head is detached from the body, both of them will die" (87). "At some point," she says, "my neck must have closed over, pond freezing or a wound, shutting me into my head...." (121)

The division of the self is, at least partly, "a trick done with mirrors." In Atwood's novel and in much of her poetry, the mirror becomes a symbol of the split self, and one's own reflection functions like a kind of negative doppelgänger. Presumably, the mirror provides a distorted image of the self, thus stealing one's sense of a real or complete self, robbing one of an identity. Anna, that character in *Surfacing* who has no self left to lose, whose identity has been lost in her preoccupation with the false, made-up self in the mirror, has become "closed in the gold compact" (203). In order to see herself as whole, the protagonist ultimately realizes, she must "stop being in the mirror." The mirror must be turned to the wall so that its reflection will not intrude between "my eyes and vision." She wishes, finally, "not to see myself but to see" (203). In the poem "Tricks with Mirrors" Atwood considers the dangers of perceiving reflection rather than whatever reality might exist, and concludes: "It is not a trick either, / It is a craft: / mirrors are crafty."[3] It is interesting at this point to recall that in Brontë's *Jane Eyre*, Jane's first visual contact with the mad Bertha, her doppelgänger, is a reflection in a mirror.

The camera is another device which Atwood sees as

revealing the split self or doppelgänger, the "not me but the missing part of me" (124). Cameras, like mirrors, according to Atwood's protagonist, can also steal the soul, as the Indians believed. Like "toilets and vacuum cleaners," other examples of "logic become visible," cameras might operate to "make people vanish," stealing "not only your soul but your body also" (136). Photographs serve to shut one in "behind the paper" (124).

As products of the world of logic, cameras are always operated by men in Atwood's works. The fiancé in *The Edible Woman*,[4] for example, is a camera enthusiast. When he explodes his flash attachment in the eyes of the protagonist, she runs for her psychological life. In *Surfacing*, David and Joe complete their victimization of Anna by what amounts to a form of rape as they coerce her into revealing her naked body before their intrusive, phallic movie camera, which they use against her "like a bazooka or a strange instrument of torture" (156). The protagonist considers herself reprieved in having evaded the movie camera, and, ultimately, she demonstrates a superior wisdom by emptying the footage of movie film into the lake. But those characters in Atwood's works who victimize others with cameras are themselves victims of faulty vision. David perhaps more than Joe sees reality only through a lens, which clouds and distorts. Perhaps it is also symbolic of a lack of vision that the protagonist's father is associated with cameras; it is the weight of a camera which prevents his drowned body from "surfacing."

Cameras and mirrors thus serve to make the self more vulnerable by emphasizing its division, but the doppelgänger or missing part of the self is also detectable by other means. Anna, employing a perverted version of the magic which is part of Atwood's representation of the female principle, reads the protagonist's palm. She

perceives that some of the lines are double and asks, "Do
you have a twin?" (8) The protagonist's twin, of course,
is that part of herself which is alienated, suppressed,
and almost irretrievably lost.

Part of that lost self is an artist who compromised and
became an illustrator, acting on the advice that "there
has never been any important women artists" (58). All
Canadian artists, according to Atwood, suffer a kind of
schizophrenia. In *Survival,* Atwood's exploration of
Canadian literature and the Canadian psyche, she
writes:

> We speak of isolated people as being "cut off," but in
> fact something is cut off from them; as artists, deprived
> of audience and cultural tradition, they are mutilated. If
> your arm or leg has been cut off you are a cripple, if your
> tongue has been cut off you are a mute, if part of your
> brain has been removed you are an idiot or an amnesiac,
> if your balls have been cut off you are a eunuch or a
> *castrato*. . . . Artists have suffered emotional and artistic
> death at the hands of an indifferent or hostile audience.[5]

The subject of the protagonist's illustrations is, significantly, children's fairy tales. "I can imitate anything,"
she declares (59). She does not, however, imitate reality,
but rather she creates a fantasy world with her sketches
of idealized princesses and unconvincing giants. She
also has created a fairy tale for her own history, the facts
of which are obscured even in her own mind. Thus, she
has lost a part of herself somewhere between memory
and lie. She fears the truth, but also fears losing it, as she
takes inventory of her memories. "I'll start inventing
them and then there will be no way of correcting it, the
ones who could help are gone. I run quickly over my
version of it, my life, checking it like an alibi" (82).

For example, she has invented the alibi of an unsuccessful marriage[6] and a childbirth to sublimate the more
painful fact that she unwillingly underwent an abortion

and was then abandoned by a complacent, middle-aged lover. Fragments of memory of the abortion itself—often described in terms of amputation, cutting, splitting—cause such pain that she cannot accept their reality. She considers that her invented son, in reality an aborted fetus, is "sliced off from me like a Siamese twin, my own flesh canceled" (54). But it is an unborn child who represents her twin, a part of her self, and she is haunted by unbidden visions of the abortion which symbolizes her division from herself:

> I knew when it was, it was in a bottle curled up, staring out at me like a cat pickled; it had huge jelly eyes and fins instead of hands, fish gills, I couldn't let it out, it was dead already, it had drowned in air (163).

The abortion itself, however, is not a cause for but an effect of the protagonist's split psyche. If a complete self had been in control, she is ultimately to realize, the operation would never have occurred. In order to become an autonomous, completed self, however, the protagonist must heal yet another kind of split—that between "good" and "evil." She must come to terms with herself as perpetrator as well as victim, or at least as a correspondent in her own victimization. During an interview, Atwood explained her protagonist's problem in the following way:

> If you define yourself as intrinsically innocent, then you have a lot of problems, because in fact you aren't. And the thing with her is she wishes not to be human. She wishes to be not human, because being human inevitably involves being guilty, and if you define yourself as innocent, you can't accept that.[7]

Atwood's concern with this delusion of female innocence is also reflected in other of her works. Marian in *The Edible Woman*, for example, maintains her own innocence throughout a destructive sexual relationship until the very end when she realizes that she, too, is guilty of exploitation and destruction. In *Survival*, Atwood groups the subjects of Canadian literature into what she terms "basic Victim Positions."[8] She states that the central question in Canadian literature is: "Who is responsible?"[9] The answer to that question, provided most clearly in *Surfacing*, is that ultimate responsibility lies almost inevitably in the self. Like Lessing's Martha Quest Hesse in *The Four-Gated City* confronting the "self-hater," that part of the self which victimizes both the self and others, Atwood's protagonist must confront her own complicity in such acts as the abortion. Carol P. Christ, in her article "Margaret Atwood: The Surfacing of Women's Spiritual Quest and Vision," upholds a similar contention:

> Her association of power with evil and her dissociation of herself from both reflect a typical female delusion of innocence, which hides her complicity in evil and feeds her fake belief that she can do nothing but witness her victimization. In order to regain her power the protagonist must realize that she does not live in a world where only others have power to do evil.[10]

Even God, or perhaps most especially God, the protagonist comes to realize, incorporates evil: "If the Devil was allowed a tail and horns, God needed them also, they were advantages" (181).

In searching her childhood for the self she has lost and the memories of evil which she has unconsciously suppressed, the protagonist comes across two scrapbooks preserved by her mother. One contains drawings by her brother, all depicting war, bomber planes decorated with swastikas, people under torture—all obvious symbols for what the protagonist sees as male power in its most evil form. Her own drawings, in contrast, are representations of an impossible innocence, a feminine vision of fertility represented by artificial Easter heavens of bunnies and eggs and colored grass. The male and female principles, always in perfect balance in these childish drawings, are represented by a moon in the upper left hand corner and a sun in the right. A more enlightened, adult protagonist recalls:

> I didn't want there to be wars and death, I wanted them not to exist; only rabbits with their colored egg houses, sun and moon orderly above the flat earth, summer always, I wanted everyone to be happy. But his pictures were more accurate, the weapons, the disintegrating soldiers: he was a realist, that protected him (151).

At another point in her memory gathering, the protagonist recalls her brother's childhood occupation of capturing and imprisoning wild animals and insects, and then allowing them to die. Her own "feminine" role was to free the animals, risking her brother's anger. A memory which is less congenial to her self-delusion of feminine innocence involves her cooperation with her brother in an act which foreshadows her cooperation in the abortion, the stabbing and dismembering of a doll, left then to float, mutilated, in the lake.

For the protagonist, the brother thus represents male power in general, manifesting itself in war games and in the violation of an essentially feminine nature, the wilderness. His exploitation of animals is repeated in the actions of "the Americans," hunters and fishermen who come to Canada to gratuitously destroy for sport. The Americans represent society's destruction of nature, obvious even in the Canadian backwoods as pollution and land "development" encroach upon the island sanctuary which is the protagonist's home. Americans, she says, "spread themselves like a virus" (148). They represent power: "Straight power, they mainlined it. . . . The innocents get slaughtered because they exist" (147). Finally, the Americans are manifestations of that origin of evil, the Hitler-boogie of the protagonist's childhood. They call to mind the fascist figure as sexual oppressor in the works of Woolf and Lessing.

Atwood's symbolism involving nature as victim is, quite obviously, multilayered. The protagonist, like the exploited wilderness, represents Canada itself and its predicament as a political victim. As Brontë, Woolf, Lessing, and Laing have also maintained and as has been discussed in each of the preceding chapters, individual schizophrenia is often a reflection of a greater, more pernicious national schizophrenia. Atwood's protagonist is a divided self, as Canada is a country divided and exploited by Americans. Atwood writes in the afterword to *The Journals of Susanna Moodie*: "If the national mental illness of the United States is megalomania, that of Canada is paranoid schizophrenia."[11]

The representative crime of the Americans in *Surfacing* is the killing of a heron, slaughtered not for food but in truth merely because "it exists." The bird, as a trophy of power, is hanged from a tree, wings outspread, in crucifixion position. The protagonist sees the heron as symbolic of her own psychological death, but sees herself as free of responsibility for both the heron's and her own fate. She is to learn, however, that the "Americans" are, in reality, Canadians, like herself, and thus she too is somehow guilty, involved. Through her passivity in refusing to prevent the heron's death, she has cooperated in its execution, very much in the same way that she has cooperated in the perpetration of the abortion. Of the heron's death she says, "I felt a sickening complicity, sticky as glue, blood on my hands, as though I had been there and watched without saying No or doing anything to stop it" (150). Later in the novel, she says of her participation in the abortion: "Instead of granting it sanctuary, I let them catch it. I could have said No but I didn't; that made me one of them, too, a killer" (165).

Thus the exploiter is not "they" but "we"; women too

are human and therefore killers—but perhaps with
some mitigation. The protagonist kills animals only for
food and then only with a kind of religious reverence
for the creature she has destroyed. She fantasizes, as she
clubs a flailing fish on the back of the head or fastens a
squealing frog onto a fish hook, that the animals will
their own victimization just as people do and are willing
to die to sustain her: "They had chosen to die and for-
given me in advance" (72). Later, she thinks:

> The shape of the heron flying above us the first evening
> we fished, legs and neck stretched, wings outspread, a
> blue-gray cross, and the other heron or was it the same
> one, hanging wrecked from the tree. Whether it died
> willingly, consented, whether Christ died willingly, any-
> thing that suffers and dies instead of us is Christ; if they
> didn't kill birds and fish they would have killed us. The
> animals die that we may live, they are substitute people,
> hunters in the fall killing the deer, that is Christ also.
> And we eat them out of cans or otherwise; we are eaters
> of death, dead Christ-flesh resurrecting inside us, grant-
> ing us life. Canned Spam, canned Jesus. . . . (160)

It is perhaps her delusive claim to innocence, and thus
her lack of reverence, which prevents Marian in *The
Edible Woman* from eating meat and, later in the novel,
from eating almost anything at all. Only when she recognizes her complicity in her own victimization, when
she understands that she has allowed men to "eat" or
destroy her and that she has also attempted to destroy
them, can Marian overcome her antipathy to food, bake
a huge cake which is an effigy of herself, and gobble it
down.

The traditional greeting of the fishermen in *Surfacing*, "Getting any?", is also a sexual allusion. The violation of nature by society is, for Atwood's protagonist,
paradigmatic of the violation of women by men. Sexual
politics, too, she sees as a battle, with herself as victim.
The protagonist recalls her childhood arguments with

her brother in which "after a while I no longer fought back because I never won. The only defense was flight, invisibility" (155).

More victimized in sexual politics than the protagonist, who at least intuits something of her complicity in her situation, is Anna, whose "invisibility" is achieved behind her excessively applied cosmetics and the smoke from her constant cigarette. Her only reading material is murder mysteries, though she never realizes the ironic fact that she herself is a victim of another sort of murder. In Anna's relationship with David, her body is "her only weapon and she was fighting for her life, he was her life, her life was the fight: she was fighting him because if she ever surrendered the balance of power would be broken and he would go elsewhere. To continue the war" (175). Anna says of David's tyranny over her: "He's got this little set of rules. If I break one of them I get punished, except he keeps changing them so I'm never sure" (141). David, thus, is uncontestably the winner as Anna masochistically endures, perhaps even enjoys, his crude and insulting sexual allusions, his insistence on her stupidity, her own reduction as a human being.

The protagonist, perhaps, has chosen her mate a bit more wisely. Joe is more "natural" than civilized, more animal than man, with his exceptionally hairy body and his inability to communicate verbally: "Everything I value about him seems to be physical: the rest is either unknown, disagreeable or ridiculous" (67). "What will preserve him," she says at another point, "is the absence of words" (181). Joe's ability to manipulate power, too, is limited, as indicated by his professional failure as a potter whose grotesque vases no one ever buys. "Perhaps it's not only his body I like," the protagonist thinks, "perhaps it's his failure; that also has a kind of purity" (64). Finally, Joe is desirable because "he isn't anything, he

is only half formed, and for that reason I can trust him"
(223).

But even Joe, for a time, insists on commitment,
"love" and marriage. For the protagonist, with the living
proof provided by Anna and David constantly before
her, marriage is more a surrender than a commitment;
it is, for the woman, total immersion in the male world
and thus a further division of the female self. One
ceases, in marriage, to be a whole self and turns "into
part of a couple" (44). The protagonist thinks of her
imagined former marriage as "like jumping off a cliff.
That was the feeling I had all the time I was married; in
the air, going down, waiting for the smash at the bot-
tom" (53). Married people, she thinks, are like the
wooden man and woman in the barometer she saw
when she was little, balancing each other in a perpetual
kind of opposition.

Marriage and sex, for Atwood much as for Brontë,
Woolf, and Lessing, are linked not only to the
psychological death of the self, but to physical death as
well. Atwood's protagonist perhaps confuses childbirth
and abortion, but the process is nonetheless grotesque.
"They take the baby out with a fork like a pickle out of a
jar. After that they fill your veins up with red plastic, I
saw it running down through the tube, I won't let them
do that to me ever again" (92). Contraception in itself
poses a very real and practical danger. The protagonist
discusses with Anna the adverse and potentially lethal
effects of "the pill" on women's bodies. It is diabolic that
pills come in "moon-shaped" packages, masquerading
as feminine creations, because, like cameras, they are
inventions of male logic. Also, like cameras, they act to
obscure vision, covering the eye with a film like vaseline.
The protagonist concludes:

> Love without fear, sex without risk, that's what they
> wanted to be true; and they almost pulled it off, but as in

> magicians' tricks or burglaries half-success is failure and
> we're back to the other things. Love is taking precau-
> tions. . . . Sex used to smell like rubber gloves and now it
> does again, no more handy green plastic packages,
> moon-shaped so that the woman can pretend she's still
> natural, cyclical, instead of a chemical slot machine. But
> soon they'll have the artificial womb, I wonder how I feel
> about that (91–92).

Later, as she overhears Anna's strangled cries and inhuman moans through the thin walls of the cabin, the
protagonist thinks that sex is "like death" (94). Love and
sex as destructive forces are also themes in Atwood's
poetry: "next time we commit / love, we ought to /
choose in advance what to kill."[12] By the conclusion of
Surfacing, however, the protagonist is able to understand that sex includes life as well as death, that it can, at
least theoretically, be natural and positive as well as
mechanical and destructive.

In the meantime, however, the protagonist is still
divided, unable to achieve any resolution of such opposites as life and death, creation and destruction. She
fears sexual commitment and so elects the defensive
mechanism of refusing to "feel." A similar technique,
described in the foregoing chapters, is used by Woolf's
Septimus Warren Smith and Clarissa Dalloway and by
Lessing's Martha Quest Hesse. The first indication that
Atwood's protagonist has chosen such a procedure is
her dispassionate, almost journalistic narrative report-
ing of events and developments. "Anesthesia," she says,
"that's one technique. . . ." (13) Most often, however,
she does not accept the responsibility for her inability to
feel, classing it as a kind of congenital condition or birth
defect: "Perhaps I'd been like that all my life, just as
some babies are born deaf or without a sense of touch"
(121). But as she observes her companions, hears their
"canned laughter," and realizes that they too are incapable of feeling, she thinks "or perhaps we are normal

and the ones who can love are freaks, they have an extra
organ, like the vestigial eye in the foreheads of amphib-
ians they've never found the use for" (157).

Another protective technique, one discussed at some
length in the chapter on Lessing, is the depersonalization of sex. Atwood takes the idea to its extreme absur-
dity: "two people making love with paper bags over their
heads, not even any eyeholes. Would that be good or
bad?" (76) But, she imagines, if sex and marriage could
be relegated to the inconsequential, the trivial, they
could not perhaps claim so many victims. Marriage, says
the protagonist, is "like playing Monopoly or doing
crossword puzzles" (100); moving in with Joe is "more
like buying a gold fish or a potted cactus plant, not
because you want one in advance but because you happen to be in the store and you see them lined up on the
counter" (47). Even relationships with other women are
superficial; the protagonist has known Anna only two
months, yet she is "my best woman friend" (10).

Such procedures as refusing to feel and to relate to
other people, however, limit and divide the self almost
as effectively as the dangers they minimize. The protagonist longs for the ability to feel: "I rehearsed emo-
tions, naming them: joy, peace, guilt, release, love and
hate, react, relate; what to feel was like what to wear,
you watched others and memorized it" (128). The protagonist has even resorted to pricking herself with pins
to experience at least a physical feeling: "They've discovered rats prefer any sensation to none. The insides
of my arms were stippled with tiny wounds, like an
addict's" (129).

Coincidental with the inability to feel is the protagonist's inability to communicate. The very language,
for her, becomes useless and finally undesirable: "Language divides us into fragments" (167). In replying to
Joe's proposal of marriage, she finds "the words were

coming out of me like the mechanical words from a talking doll, the kind with the pull tape at the back; the whole speech was unwinding, everything in order, a spool" (100). In order to ever communicate again, the protagonist thinks that she must find a language of her own:

> I was seeing poorly, translating badly, a dialect problem. I should have used my own. In the experiments they did with children, shutting them up with deaf-and-dumb nurses, locking them in closets, depriving them of words, they found that after a certain age the mind is incapable of absorbing any language; but how could they tell the child hadn't invented one, unrecognizable to everyone but itself? (87–88).

Woolf's Septimus Warren Smith can understand the birds; Lessing's Lynda Coldridge communicates with spirits in code. Atwood's protagonist ultimately is to conclude: "The animals have no need for speech, why talk when you are a word. . . ." (210)

If one cannot communicate, cannot feel, has no name, has been so thoroughly divided, one is, like Atwood's protagonist at the beginning of the novel, psychologically dead. Atwood herself has referred to *Surfacing* as "a ghost story."[13] Her protagonist has, in the sense of Laing in *The Divided Self*,[14] been engulfed, "drowned," ceased to exist as a self, just as both her father and her aborted baby have drowned, one in the lake, the other "in air." She speaks also of her brother having drowned as an infant, an event which she has vicariously experienced, or at least somehow observed from what she describes as her mother's transparent womb. Later we learn that the brother was saved by the mother's intervention, but according to the protagonist, he has not regarded his experience with the respect it warrants; it was, the protagonist thinks, a kind of rebirth. "If it had happened to me I would have felt there was something special about me, to be raised from the dead like that; I would have returned with secrets, I would have known things most people didn't" (83).

Drowning thus comes to represent not only death or a loss of self, but also a procedure for finding the self. The protagonist's descent into the lake in search of the Indian cave paintings is symbolic of her descent into her own psyche, from which return, resurrection, "surfacing," is possible. Similarly, Lessing's Martha descends into madness before she can emerge as truly and divinely sane. *Surfacing* is as much an allegory of the quest for psychological rebirth, for life, as it is a search for the theological meaning Carol P. Christ describes.

To be "reborn," just as to be born, the protagonist must have a "gift" from both father and mother. She has carried "death around inside me, layering it over, a cyst, a tumor, black pearl" (165). To be alive, whole, she must recognize that she is a product of both the male and the female principles. She must understand her parentage and her origins before she can understand herself.

Her search for the father ends in the depths of the lake. "Return" for him is impossible; his body, weighed down by the symbolic camera, has never "surfaced." He is reduced to "a dark oval trailing limbs" (162). Like Virgil, who can guide Dante's descent and show him the way through hell but never enter paradise himself, the protagonist's father represents human reason and its limitations. He can point the way with his drawings and maps, "pictographs," to "the place of the gods," the sacred places "where you could learn the truth" (171), but he cannot himself see truth.

In the beginning, the protagonist imagines that her missing father has gone mad and lurks in the wilderness outside their cabin. His madness, she imagines, would be "like stepping through a usual door and finding yourself in a different galaxy, purple trees and red moons and a green sun" (166). Such experiences, she thinks, could lead to revelation: "He had discovered new places, new oracles, they were things he was seeing the way I had seen, true vision; at the end, after the failure of logic" (166). But it is only the protagonist herself and not her father who has such visions. In her dive deep into the lake she discovers not the cave paintings her father has described but the "galaxy" of her own psyche: "pale green pinpricks of light," strange shapes and mysterious fish, "chasm-dwellers" (162).

The father himself is incapable of such visions because, for him, logic has never failed. He represents, however, the best of the male principle—logic without destruction. He has, for himself and his children, reasoned away evil, teaching them that even Hitler, "many-tentacled, ancient and indestructible as the Devil" (148), is not, after all, "the triumph of evil but the failure of reason" (65). The father has attempted to protect his family from evil by secluding them in the Canadian wilderness where World War II is only a subject for children's games. Yet these very games reflect the failure of the father's teaching and indicate the inevitability of evil: the first pages of the novel describe the young brother and sister, their feet wrapped in blankets, pretending that "the Germans shot our feet off" (8).

As the father tries to eclipse evil, so he tries to reason away superstition, fear, religion: "Christianity was something he'd escaped from, he wished to protect us from its distortions" (61). But this too is impossible. The protagonist's childhood is haunted by the idea that "there was a dead man in the sky watching everything I did" (51). Ultimately, she must go beyond the father, beyond the world of logic which he represents. She must confront the presence of evil, in the world and in the self, and she must also confront the gods: "The power from my father's intercession wasn't enough to protect me, it gave only knowledge and there were more gods than his, his were the gods of the head, antlers rooted in the brain" (174).

The father's gift of knowledge, however, cannot be considered inconsequential. He has led the way to self-knowledge and pointed out reality. Even the father's drowned body is "something I knew about" (162); it is, symbolically, also the body of her own aborted fetus, "drowned in air," its fishlike corpse having been flushed through the sewers, "travelling... back to the sea" (163). As she recognizes her father's body, the pro-tagonist's past suddenly becomes very clear to her and her fantasy past disintegrates. "I killed it. It wasn't a child but it could have been one, I didn't allow it" (163). "It was all real enough, it was reality enough for ever...." (164) With this recognition the protagonist begins to experience feeling, life: "Feeling was begin-ning to seep back into me, I tingled like a foot that's been asleep" (166–67). Shortly afterward she finds that she is even able to cry. But her resurrection is not yet complete: "I wanted to be whole" (167).

The father thus participates in a kind of conception, but the actual birth process is the business of the female. In order to be reborn, to become whole, the protagonist must also find a "gift" from her dead mother:

> It would be right for my mother to have left something for me also, a legacy. His was complicated, tangled, but hers would be simple as a hand, it would be final. I was not completed yet; there had to be a gift from each of them (170–71).

The mother's legacy is the revelation of a drawing from the protagonist's childhood of a woman "with a round moon stomach: the baby was sitting up inside gazing out" (180–81), just as the protagonist has earlier en-visioned herself as present before her birth, able to see the world through her mother's transparent womb.

The protagonist interprets the message of the drawing as an instruction: in order to be alive and whole she must replace, resurrect, that part of herself which she has killed—the aborted fetus and the fertility aspect of the female principle which it represents. Early in the novel the protagonist has found it "impossible to be like my mother" (58); now she must *become* her mother, "the miraculous double woman" (205), giving birth to herself as well as to new life. The protagonist thus seeks out her lover and takes him to the shore of the lake, carefully arranging their positions so that the moon, representing the female principle as in the childhood drawings, is on her left hand and the absent male sun on her right. According to Carol P. Christ the conception itself is a religious act: "As she conceives, the protagonist resembles the Virgin Mother goddesses of old: at one with her sexual power, she is complete in herself; the male is incidental."[15] The conception is also, however, a psychological rebirth, a healing of the divided self:

> He trembles and then I can feel my lost child surfacing within me, forgiving me, rising from the lake where it had been prisoned so long, its eyes and teeth phosphorescent; the two halves clasp, interlocking like fingers, it buds, it sends out fronds (187).

Whereas images of cutting, splitting, division, fragmentation have dominated the novel to this point, now images of unity, joining, completeness begin to supercede. The protagonist has united the two halves of herself, found her parentage, reconciled the male and female principles within the self. Thus the "two halves" of herself also "clasp, interlocking like fingers." The body, which has been for her "even scarier than god" (50), has been integrated with the head: "I'm not against the body or the head either; only the neck which creates the illusion that they are separate" (87). For a second time the protagonist refers to palmistry: "When the heartline and the headline are one ... you are either a criminal, an idiot or a saint" (181). Now saintlike, in the sense that Woolf's Septimus is a saint, Atwood's protagonist has also resolved within herself the opposites of life and death. Thus she reflects nature itself:

> I lie down on the bottom of the canoe and wait. The still water gathers the heat; birds, off in the forest a woodpecker, somewhere a thrush. Through the trees the sun glances; the swamp around me smolders, energy of decay turning to growth, green fire. I remember the heron; by now it will be insects, frogs, fish, other herons. My body sends out filaments in me; I ferry it secure between death and life, I multiply (194).

Although the argument for androgynous vision may be made with some relevancy in the case of Virginia Woolf, it is not a meaningful concept when applied to Atwood. For Atwood even more than for Woolf the male principle is ultimately expendable. The female principle alone and in itself incorporates and resolves opposites. Life and death, good and evil, exist within the protagonist, within all women, as they exist in nature. Atwood has described nature in *Survival* as being, not benevolently motherlike or nurselike in the Wordsworthian sense, but rather as a living process "which includes opposites: life and death, 'gentleness' and 'hostility.'"[16] She invariably associates the female principle with nature; she deals, not with nature as a woman, but rather with women as nature. Therefore, although nature is not a mother in Atwood's novel, the protagonist's mother is aligned with nature, at home with it as with an extension of herself. Almost witchlike, with her long hair and wearing her magically powerful leather jacket, the mother feeds wild birds from her hand, charms a bear, and is in tune with the seasons which she carefully records in a special diary. It is she and not the father who represents life as she gives birth, saves her drowning son, prohibits cruelty; yet, dying herself, she also understands the mysteries of death. The protagonist, as a child asking about death, is convinced that her mother "had the answers but wouldn't tell" (83). The protagonist recalls her mother's own death and wishes she might have taken her from the hospital room to die in the forest. There, perhaps, she might have been reborn, like nature itself: "It sprang up from the earth, pure joy, pure death, burning white like snow" (172). It is only the male world of logic which insists on the finality of death. "The reason they invented coffins, to lock the dead in, to preserve them, they put makeup on them; they didn't want them spreading or changing into anything else. The stone with the name and the date was on them to weight them down" (171).

Like her mother, the protagonist, although she hardly realizes it, is also aligned with nature, acting as guide for her companions in the backwoods and insuring their survival. She is instinctively aware of the dangers of the wilderness; she knows how to catch a fish and balance a canoe. She is even immune from the insects which so plague the others.

The protagonist is truly a part of nature, able to incorporate its powers into herself, however, only after she has received her mother's legacy and conceived both herself and her child. Her next act is to reject the world of male logic, the elements of civilization, its canned food and its clothing and its values. "Everything from history must be eliminated," she says, as she burns and tears books, clothing, even her fake wedding ring. The cabin itself is unbearable because it is man-made, and so she enters the forest naked except for a blanket which she will need "until the fur grows" (206).

Here she can experience her own birth:

> My back is on the sand, my head rests against the rock, innocent as plankton; my hair spreads out, moving and

> fluid in the water. The earth rotates, holding my body
> down to it as it holds the moon; the sun pounds in the
> sky, red flames and rays pulsing from it, searing away
> the wrong form that encases me, dry rain soaking
> through me, warming the blood egg I carry. I dip my
> head beneath the water, washing my eyes....
>   When I am clean I come up out of the lake, leaving my
> false body floated on the surface.... (206)

Now in tune with the powers of nature, the protagonist is granted a series of visions, one of prehistory itself: "The forest leaps upward, enormous, the way it was before they cut it, columns of sunlight frozen; the boulders float, melt, everything is made of water" (210) She also sees her mother, who has always been "ten thousand years behind the rest" (58), and who is also an extension of eternal nature. The protagonist *becomes* her mother, placing her feet in the footprints left by the vision, and finding "that they are my own" (217). Thus she too is synonomous with nature: "I am not an animal or a tree, I am the thing in which the trees and animals move and grow, I am a place" (210).

In this mystical identification with nature and with the female principle it represents, the protagonist surrenders individual human identity. In so doing, she comes face to face with the world beyond logic. "Logic," she says, "is like a wall"; in tearing down this wall she finds "on the other side is terror" (202). Once the wall is destroyed, however, there is no choice: "From any rational point of view I am absurd; but there are no longer any rational points of view" (198). She confronts madness personified, the ultimate mirror:

> It is what my father saw, the thing you meet when you've
> stayed here too long alone.
>   I'm not frightened, it's too dangerous for me to be
> frightened of it; it gazes at me for a time with its yellow
> eyes, Wolf's eyes, depthless but lambent as the eyes of
> animals seen at night in the car headlight. Reflectors
> (216).

In *Survival*, Atwood discusses the theme of "bushing" in Canadian literature and the fascination of Canadian authors with the madness which occurs when one merges human identity with nature.[17]

But for the protagonist the descent into madness, into the "chasm" of experience, must be temporary and therapeutic, rather than permanent. She desires survival, and she knows, for example, that what society sees as insanity might well serve as an excuse for persecution; she might be victimized, like the heron:

> They can't be trusted. They'll mistake me for a human being, a naked woman wrapped in a blanket: possibly that's what they've come here for, if it's running around loose, ownerless, why not take it. They won't be able to tell what I really am. But if they guess my true form, identity, they will shoot me or bludgeon in my skull and hang me up by the feet from a tree (212).

Society is incapable of recognizing that what they perceive as a mad woman is, in reality, "only a natural woman, state of nature" (220).

Thus the protagonist, like Lessing's Martha, loses a tenuous identity only to gain a firmer one. She "surfaces" from the illogical to return to a world of logic, but not now, as before, divided, incapable of coping. Their purpose accomplished, father and mother, as principles of nature and as "gods," have reassumed their humanity and the vision has faded. "No total salvation, resurrection. Our father, our mother, I pray, Reach down for me, but it won't work: they dwindle, grow, become what they were, human" (220). There are "no gods to help me now" (219). Even nature's power is now benign, impersonal: "The lake is quiet, the trees surround me, asking and giving nothing" (224). Like Jane Eyre, Atwood's protagonist has found the mother within herself. Secure in an undivided self, the protagonist no longer needs parents or gods; she recognizes her own power and the fact that she can refuse victimization. "This above all, to refuse to be a victim. Unless I can do that I can do nothing" (222). Now even "the Americans" can be managed and seen in perspective: "They must be dealt with, but possibly they can be watched and predicted and stopped without being copied" (219). As Carol P. Christ says, the protagonist is "awakening from a male-defined world, to the greater terror and risk, and also the great potential healing and joy, of a world defined by the heroine's own feeling and judgment."[18]

Atwood writes in *Survival:* "A reader must face the fact that Canadian literature is undeniably sombre and negative, and that this to a large extent is both a reflection and a chosen definition of the national sensibility."[19] In its ringing affirmation, *Surfacing* is the exception to prove the rule. Withdrawal is no longer possible, says the protagonist, and "the alternative is death" (222). She chooses instead a new life and a new way of seeing. She carries a new child, a new messiah: "It might be the first one, the first true human; it must be born, allowed" (222). To the protagonist belongs the ultimate sanity: the knowledge that woman can descend, and return— sane, whole, victorious.

The Self-Created Other: Integration and Survival

> . . .
> Mother, last night I slept
> in your Bonwit Teller nightgown.
> Divided, you climbed into my head.
> There in my jabbering dream
> I heard my own angry cries
> and I cursed you, *Dame*
> *keep out of my slumber.*
> My good Dame, you are dead.
> And Mother, three stones
> slipped from your glittering eyes.
> . . .

> Anne Sexton,
> "The Division of Parts,"
> *To Bedlam and Part Way Back*

"The Angel in the House," and finds her submissive, pure, self-sacrificing, "feminine"—and dangerous. Her end must be a violent one if Woolf the artist is to survive:

> And while I was writing this review, I discovered that if I were going to review books I should need to do battle with a certain phantom. And that phantom was a woman, and when I came to know her better I called her after the heroine of a famous poem, The Angel in the House. It was she who used to come between me and my paper when I was writing reviews. It was she who bothered me and wasted my time and so tormented me that at last I killed her. . . . I turned upon her and caught her by the throat. I did my best to kill her. My excuse, if I were to be had up in a court of law, would be that I acted in self defence. Had I not killed her she would have killed me. She would have plucked the heart out of my writing.[2]

How to prevail as an authentic self against such role prescriptions, how to survive psychologically and assert individuality, are major considerations, not only in Woolf's works, but in the novels of Brontë, Lessing, and Atwood as well. Jane Eyre, Clarissa Dalloway, Martha Quest Hesse, and Atwood's protagonist of *Surfacing* all participate in a similar search for self, and each achieves a personal identity which at least partially redefines that which society has deemed to be the "nature" of woman.

The processes by which the protagonists achieve this end are also strikingly similar. They are processes which have their prototypes in the mythic patterns of spiritual journeys as well as in the procedures for psychoanalysis. Each protagonist begins her search for self in a psychological "dark wood," where she is beset by anxieties which involve feelings of division and thus of selflessness. Each sees that her identity is in danger of engulfment in the identities of other individuals or groups.

Is significant, for example, that in each novel, the

IN *Psychoanalysis and Women*, Jean Baker Miller laments what she sees as a lack of role models for the psychological growth of women.[1] The novels discussed in the foregoing chapters, however, do provide a series of portraits of women, each of whom achieves an appreciable level of self-realization, and therefore of self-actualization, despite the psychologically devastating e[ffects] of the male-supremacist societies in which e[ach] protagonist lives and in which women are often vi[ctims] and lunatics—losers in the war of sexual politics.

Brontë, Woolf, Lessing, and Atwood all co[ndemn] those social systems, both political and priva[te,] demand adherence to arbitrarily established [roles,] thus denying individual freedom and con[tributing to] psychological fragmentation, alienation, a[nd...] Each novelist indicates that women in p[articular suffer] from more or less obvious forms of schi[zophrenia,] constantly torn between male society's [demands for] female behavior, their own tendencie[s toward inter-] nalization of these roles, and a nos[talgia for a] more authentic self.

Virginia Woolf, in her e[ssay on "Professions for] Women," describes her perso[nal encounter with a] false self who meets the [socially] stereotyped standard for wo[men...]

protagonist undergoes some traumatic realization that she is without a name, that is, an identity. Jane Eyre reacts with fear to being called "Jane Rochester" because the change in name threatens her sense of self. Clarissa Dalloway, in the title of Woolf's novel, is denied her given name. Lessing's Martha Quest Hesse repeatedly reflects on the fact that names are meaningless for women, since they are all male-derived, whether from husband or father. Lessing's explanation provides one of the possible reasons why Atwood's protagonist remains nameless throughout *Surfacing*.

All four protagonists react to such psychologically threatening situations by adopting some form of withdrawal, whether emotional or sexual. Jane Eyre's chastity, as I have shown, reflects her desire for self preservation rather than any frigidity in her nature. A similar emphasis on sexual withdrawal is noted throughout *Mrs. Dalloway*, again the motivation being the preservation of privacy and thus a hold on ontological security, however tenuous. Lessing's protagonist, on the other hand, finds emotional safety in numbers, her multiple sexual unions serving to protect her from the vulnerability she feels when attached to one man. Marriage, in Lessing's works most particularly, threatens annihilation, physical and psychological. Atwood's protagonist attempts to preserve a sense of self by relegating her sexual relationship to the inconsequential, refusing to "feel" on either a physical or emotional level. The important consideration here is that none of these characters is asexual or unloving or dispassionate, charges frequently brought by traditional critics. Not one of the protagonists wishes to live in a world without men, although each realizes the dangers to identity which women experience in sexual relationships with men in a man's world.

Each protagonist either begins by realizing, or comes

to a conscious recognition later in the novel, that she has lost a self somewhere among the socially prescribed false selves which she has assumed, willingly or unwillingly, consciously or subconsciously. In panic at this realization, she searches for some rationale, some agent or helper to heal the divided self—a mother. The protagonist inevitably finds, whether in an actual mother or in some other figure, a mirror image of her own split psyche, a doppelgänger who is a manifestation of her schizophrenia.

It is only through recognition of this doppelgänger and thus the confrontation with one's mirror-self that the psyche can be diagnosed as split. In these novels, then, the doppelgänger serves an essentially positive function and is therefore a departure from the figure of the demonic double traditional in psychological works of fiction by male writers like Dostoevsky or Poe. Most obviously in the novels of Brontë, Lessing, and Atwood, the doppelgänger is depicted in terms of what Florence Howe has seen in relation to women poets as "the wild and holy woman."[3] She acts as a guide in the exploration of the wild places of the self, the acceptance of which is always crucial. Even Woolf's Septimus Warren Smith fits into this pattern: while male, he is nevertheless female in his psyche, and, like the doppelgängers of the other novels, is portrayed as wild, mad, and holy.

Upon recognition of the doppelgänger, each protagonist begins a descent into actual madness, or at least into the vicarious experience of madness as is the case with Jane Eyre and Clarissa Dalloway. Having descended, symbolically, into the flames where she consciously recognizes herself as "insane" or potentially insane, each protagonist, phoenixlike, is able to surface as sane, equipped with an integrated self, an identity. It is this sense of identity which then permits her to cope effectively with what continues to be, nevertheless, an essentially hostile world.

In order for such a self-integration to occur, the doppelgänger, who has represented the self as split, must in some way be annihilated or at least relegated to obscurity. Mad Bertha jumps to her death in *Jane Eyre* as does Septimus Warren Smith in *Mrs. Dalloway*. Lynda in *The Four-Gated City* disappears for a time and is later reported to have died. The mother in *Surfacing*, who functions as one of many doppelgängers but who is certainly the most important as a guide toward self-integration, is, conveniently, already dead. In the same way, women writers from Jane Austen to Sylvia Plath and beyond have annihilated, ignored, or rendered ridiculous the mothers of their major characters. The doppelgänger, like the mother, is valuable while she is an ally against the male world and while she is useful in the process of self-integration, but once her essence has been incorporated into the now integrated self, she necessarily, if tragically, becomes expendable. Thus women, quite literally perhaps, *become* their mothers.

Characters in fiction by women are not always so successful in their attempts to assimilate or annihilate the doppelgänger, and thus they fail in the quest for self-integration. One feels certain, for example, that the protagonist of Charlotte Perkins Gilman's "The Yellow Wallpaper"[4] is hopelessly lost. Gilman's story is the account of a nineteenth-century American woman's discovery of a bizarre double trapped behind the wallpaper of her bedroom. The doppelgänger in this story clearly represents not only the protagonist's own divided self but all women who are imprisoned, bound and inhibited by a society which insists that women are childlike, merely decorative, and incapable of self-actualization. The wallpaper itself, like the social conventions it symbolizes, is hideously ugly, its color a poisonous yellow and its nightmare pattern impossible to trace or even define. Any attempt to impose reason on such a torturous pattern results in madness.

Gilman's protagonist-narrator does go mad, unable to find a self among the social roles she has assumed. She longs to express a self through writing, but she has no self other than the child, the mindless infant she has become. The upper room to which she is ultimately confined by her husband, whose authority is compounded by the fact that he is a physician, is ironically described as a former nursery. It is outfitted with iron rings as in a gymnasium, barred windows to prevent accidents, and a bed bolted to the floor. The wallpaper is torn in chunks as if by children's carelessness.

Or, the reader comes to realize, maybe this room has always been a place of confinement for mad persons. Perhaps it is the narrator herself who, although she does not realize it, has always been here, "creeping" about the room until her own shoulder has left the groove she notices in the wallpaper. Perhaps the gnawed places on the bed frame are the marks of her own teeth. The protagonist's frantic attempts to free the woman from the barred wallpaper are but the struggles to free herself.

Gilman's story, unlike the novels of Brontë, Woolf, Lessing, or Atwood, does not end in even a semblance of return to sanity; it stands, rather, as a political statement, a testament to the victimization of women by society.

Among more recent women protagonists who also seem always to be in trouble, tortured by conflict and division, is Sylvia Plath's Esther Greenwood of *The Bell Jar*. Early in the novel, Esther attempts to analyze what is virtually a paralysis of the mind:

> I saw my life branching out before me like the green
> fig tree in the story. . . .
> I saw myself sitting in the crotch of this fig tree, starv-
> ing to death just because I couldn't make up my mind
> which of the figs I would choose. I wanted each and
> every one of them, but choosing one meant losing all the
> rest, and, as I sat there, unable to decide, the figs began
> to wrinkle and go black, and, one by one, they plopped
> to the ground at my feet.[5]

This division of the self and the inability to decide
who *she* is are both the cause and effect of Esther's mental breakdown. And, as in the novels discussed in the
foregoing chapters, the sense of division manifests itself
in the recognition of a doppelgänger, a mad woman
called Joan who ultimately destroys herself and whose
thoughts and feelings seem to Esther "a wry, black
image of my own." "Sometimes," Esther says, "I won-
dered if I had made Joan up" (179).

Like Lessing's Martha Quest Hesse, Esther experiments in assumed identities. Esther's "Elly Higginbot-
tom," however, is but a parody of Martha's serious, ultimately therapeutic search for the boundaries of identity. Esther, finally, is left isolated and restricted, never
seeing the physical world as beautiful in the way Lessing's Martha does. To Esther, the world is ugly and
distorted by the perimeters of the bell jar of psychosis,
where she remains "stewing in my own sour air" (152).

Esther shares with Martha, with Woolf's sympathetic
characters in *Mrs. Dalloway*, and with Atwood's protagonist in *Surfacing* a sense of victimization by a world
made up of male dominators, associated in each novel
with the image of the German fascist. The fact that
Esther's dead father was German, like Plath's own
father, compounds the association of maleness and
powerfully coercive authority. While the protagonists of
Woolf, Lessing, and Atwood, to varying extents, are all

able to combat or at least withdraw from this spectre, Esther succumbs as its victim. She repeatedly identifies herself with the Rosenbergs, who symbolize for her the Jew as scapegoat. Plath also makes such identifications in much of her poetry: in "Daddy," she writes, "Every woman adores a fascist, / The boot in the face."[6]

Perhaps Esther is but another self for Plath, who, as her poetry indicates and as biographies tell us, never found her own way back from psychosis. Elizabeth Hardwick in *Seduction and Betrayal* describes Plath as "both heroine and author; when the curtain goes down, it is her own dead body there on the stage, sacrificed to her plot."[7]

Like Plath and like the authors discussed in the previous chapters, many women writers have been and still are preoccupied with similar themes of victimization, alienation, and psychological fragmentation. Women writers of the future will undoubtedly continue to be so preoccupied, given the historically documented and continuing oppression of women as individuals. Such oppression is but a manifestation of what R. D. Laing has characterized throughout his works as society's own pervasive mental sickness, symptomized by its necessity to create categories and assign roles, its predilection to inhibit and control those who reject or would modify such roles.

Laing, as well as the majority of women writers, do not hold out much hope for society's cure. Brontë and Woolf both council withdrawal from its evils. Lessing sees the survival of the individual as dependent on nothing less than society's catastrophic destruction. Even Atwood, whose affirmation is a daring one, cautions that society must be feared and carefully watched.

For the female individual to survive, she must recognize and reject not only the pathology of social and sexual arrangements but her own participation in these arrangements as well. The protagonists of Brontë, Woolf, Lessing, and Atwood ultimately achieve such a recognition. Each affirms, at the end, a superior sanity based on personal order and the discovery of at least the potential for an authentic and integrated self.

NOTES
SELECTED BIBLIOGRAPHY
INDEX

NOTES

INTRODUCTION

1 Germaine Greer, *The Female Eunuch* (New York: Bantam, 1972), p. 92.
2 Phyllis Chesler, *Women and Madness* (New York: Avon, 1972).
3 Karen Horney, *Feminine Psychology*, ed. Harold Kelman (New York: Norton, 1967).
4 Jean Baker Miller, ed., *Psychoanalysis and Women* (Baltimore: Penguin, 1974).
5 Kate Millett, *Sexual Politics* (New York: Doubleday, 1969), p. 241.
6 Phyllis Chesler, "Patient and Patriarch: Woman in the Psychotherapeutic Relationship," in *Woman in Sexist Society: Studies in Power and Powerlessness*, ed. Vivian Gornick and Barbara K. Moran (New York: Mentor, 1972), pp. 375-76.
7 Ibid., p. 373.
8 Naomi Weisstein, "Psychology Constructs the Female, or the Fantasy Life of the Male Psychologist," in *Women's Liberation and Literature*, ed. Elaine Showalter (New York: Harcourt Brace Jovanovich, 1971), p. 273.
9 Miller, *Psychoanalysis*, p. 381.
10 Juliet Mitchell, *Woman's Estate* (New York: Random House, 1973), p. 167.
11 Juliet Mitchell, *Psychoanalysis and Feminism: Freud, Reich, Laing and Women* (New York: Random House, 1975), p. xiii.
12 Weisstein, *Psychology*, p. 273.
13 Millett, *Sexual Politics*, p. 55.
14 Chesler, *Women and Madness*, p. 31.
15 Miller, *Psychoanalysis*, p. 379.
16 Mitchell, *Psychoanalysis and Feminism*, p. 278.
17 Elizabeth Janeway, *Man's World, Woman's Place* (New York: Dell, 1971).

131

18 Mitchell, *Psychoanalysis and Feminism*, p. xvi.
19 R. D. Laing, *The Politics of Experience* (New York: Random House, 1967), p. 79.
20 R. D. Laing, *The Divided Self* (New York: Random House, 1969), p. 25.
21 R. D. Laing, *The Politics of the Family* (New York: Random House, 1969).
22 Otto Rank, *The Double: A Psychoanalytic Study*, trans. and ed. Harry Tucker, Jr. (Chapel Hill: University of North Carolina Press, 1971).
23 Robert Rogers, *A Psychoanalytic Study of the Double in Literature* (Detroit: Wayne State University Press, 1970), p. 18.
24 Laing, *Politics of Experience*, pp. 47–48.
25 Ibid., pp. 46–47.
26 Adrienne Rich, *Of Woman Born: Motherhood as Experience and Institution* (New York: Norton, 1976).
27 Chesler, *Women and Madness*, p. 4.

"THE FRENZIED MOMENT"

1 Charlotte Brontë, *Jane Eyre*, ed. Jane Jack and Margaret Smith (London: Oxford University Press, 1969), p. 370. All subsequent references are to pages in this edition.
2 W. A. Craig, *The Brontë Novels* (London: Methuen, 1968), p. 81.
3 David Smith, "Incest Patterns in Two Victorian Novels," pt. 1, "Her Master's Voice: *Jane Eyre* and the Incest Taboo," *Literature and Psychology* 15 (Summer 1965), 136–44.
4 Richard Chase, "The Brontës: A Centennial Observance," in *The Brontës: A Collection of Critical Essays*, ed. Ian Gregor (Englewood Cliffs, N.J.: Prentice Hall, 1970), p. 25.
5 R. D. Laing, *The Politics of Experience* (New York: Random House, 1967), p. 12.
6 Helene Moglen, *Charlotte Brontë: The Self Conceived* (New York: Norton, 1976), p. 30.
7 Ibid., p. 110.
8 Ibid., p. 111.
9 Winifred Gerin, *Charlotte Brontë: The Evolution of Genius* (London: Oxford University Press, 1967), p. 278.
10 Margot Peters, *Charlotte Brontë: Style in the Novel* (Madison: University of Wisconsin Press, 1973), p. 108.
11 R. D. Laing, *The Divided Self* (New York: Random House, 1969), p. 47.
12 Ibid., p. 49.

13 Virginia Woolf, *A Room of One's Own* (New York: Harcourt, Brace and World, 1957), p. 76.

14 Margot Peters, *Unquiet Soul: A Biography of Charlotte Brontë* (New York: Doubleday, 1975), p. 95.

15 Adrienne Rich, "*Jane Eyre*: Temptations of a Motherless Woman," *MS.* 2, no. 4 (October 1973), p. 98.

16 Moglen, *Self Conceived*, p. 128.

17 Terry Eagleton, *Myths of Power: A Marxist Study of the Brontës* (London: Macmillan, 1975), p. 32.

18 Moglen, *Self Conceived*, pp. 126–27.

19 Jean Rhys, *Wide Sargasso Sea* (New York: Norton, 1966).

20 Woolf, *Room*, p. 72.

21 Kate Millett, *Sexual Politics* (New York: Doubleday, 1969), p. 140.

22 Charlotte Brontë, *Villette* (New York: Harper & Row, 1972), p. 154.

23 Ibid., p. 200.

24 Millett, *Sexual Politics*, p. 192.

25 Laing, *Divided Self*, p. 47.

26 Peters, *Unquiet Soul*, p. 19.

27 Moglen, *Self Conceived*, p. 143.

28 Carolyn Heilbrun, *Toward a Recognition of Androgyny* (New York: Alfred A. Knopf, 1973), p. 59.

29 Peters, *Style in the Novel*, p. 107.

30 Adrienne Rich, *Of Woman Born: Motherhood as Experience and Institution* (New York: Norton, 1976), pp. 252–53.

31 M. Esther Harding, *Woman's Mysteries, Ancient and Modern* (New York: Bantam, 1973), p. 70.

32 Peters, *Style in the Novel*, p. 153.

33 Moglen, *Self Conceived*, p. 21.

"THE SANE AND THE INSANE"

1 Virginia Woolf, *A Writer's Diary*, ed. Leonard Woolf (New York: Harcourt, Brace, 1954), p. 51.

2 Virginia Woolf, *Mrs. Dalloway* (New York: Harcourt, Brace & World, 1925), p. 3. All subsequent references are to pages in this edition.

3 R. D. Laing, *The Politics of Experience* (New York: Random House, 1967), p. 32.

4 Virginia Woolf, *Three Guineas* (New York: Harcourt, Brace & World, 1938), pp. 216–17.

5 E. M. Forster, "Virginia Woolf," in *Virginia Woolf: A Collection of*

Critical Essays, ed. Claire Sprague (Englewood Cliffs, N.J.: Prentice Hall, 1971), p. 22.

6 Ibid., pp. 22–23.

7 Alex Zwerdling, "*Mrs. Dalloway* and the Social System," *PMLA* 92, no. 1 (January 1977), p. 75.

8 Woolf, *Writer's Diary*, p. 56.

9 R. D. Laing, *The Divided Self* (New York: Random House, 1969), p. 15.

10 Virginia Woolf, "On Being Ill," in *Collected Essays* (New York: Harcourt, Brace and World, 1967), IV, 196.

11 Nancy Topping Bazin, *Virginia Woolf and the Androgynous Vision* (New Brunswick, N.J.: Rutgers University Press, 1973), p. 117.

12 Jeremy Hawthorn, *Virginia Woolf's Mrs. Dalloway: A Study in Alienation* (London: Sussex University Press, 1975), p. 56.

13 Ibid., p. 35.

14 Ibid., p. 94.

15 Laing, *Divided Self*, p. 45.

16 Ibid., p. 46.

17 Ibid., p. 47.

18 Morris Beja, *Epiphany in the Modern Novel* (Seattle: University of Washington Press, 1971), p. 120.

19 Laing, *Politics of Experience*, p. 89.

20 Ibid., pp. 24–25.

21 Ibid., p. 25.

22 Ibid., p. 137.

23 Woolf, *Writer's Diary*, p. 56.

24 Jean O. Love, *Worlds in Consciousness: Mythopoetic Thought in the Novels of Virginia Woolf* (Berkeley: University of California Press, 1970), p. 156.

25 Beja, *Epiphany*, p. 122.

26 James Naremore, *The World Without a Self: Virginia Woolf and the Novel* (New Haven and London: Yale University Press, 1973), p. 106.

27 Aaron Fleishman, *Virginia Woolf: A Critical Reading* (Baltimore: The Johns Hopkins University Press, 1975), p. 77.

28 Laing, *Politics of Experience*, p. 24.

29 Harvena Richter, *Virginia Woolf: The Inward Voyage* (Princeton: Princeton University Press, 1970), p. 120.

30 Laing, *Politics of Experience*, p. 36.

31 Ibid., p. 89.

32 Ibid., p. 90.

33 Ibid., p. 90.

34 Forster, "Virginia Woolf," p. 17.

A REHEARSAL FOR MADNESS

1 Doris Lessing, *The Four-Gated City* (New York: Alfred A. Knopf, 1969), p. 481. All subsequent references are to pages in this edition.
2 Marion Vlastos, "Doris Lessing and R. D. Laing: Psychopolitics and Prophecy," *PMLA* 91, no. 2 (March 1976), p. 257.
3 R. D. Laing, *The Politics of Experience* (New York: Random House, 1967), p. 49.
4 Dorothy Brewster, *Doris Lessing* (New York: Twayne Publishers, 1965), p. 13.
5 Laing, *Politics of Experience*, p. 99.
6 Ibid., p. 8.
7 Janet Sydney Kaplan, "The Limits of Consciousness in the Novels of Doris Lessing," *Contemporary Literature* 14 (1973), xiii.
8 Doris Lessing, *The Golden Notebook* (New York: Simon & Schuster, 1962), p. xiii.
9 Laing, *Politics of Experience*, p. 116.
10 Kaplan, "Limits of Consciousness," p. 546.
11 Vlastos, "Doris Lessing and R. D. Laing," p. 249.
12 Laing, *Politics of Experience*, p. 31.
13 Ibid., p. 32.
14 Virginia Woolf, *A Room of One's Own* (New York: Harcourt, Brace and World, 1957), p. 47.
15 Laing, *Politics of Experience*, p. 84.
16 Ibid., p. 93.
17 Ibid., p. xiii.
18 Ibid., p. 8.
19 Ibid., p. 36.

"AFTER THE FAILURE OF LOGIC"

1 Margaret Atwood, *Surfacing* (New York: Simon & Schuster, 1972), p. 166. All subsequent references are to pages in this edition.
2 R. D. Laing, *The Divided Self* (New York: Random House, 1969).
3 Margaret Atwood, *Selected Poems* (Toronto: Oxford University Press, 1976), p. 159.
4 Margaret Atwood, *The Edible Woman* (New York: Little Brown, 1969).
5 Margaret Atwood, *Survival: A Thematic Guide to Canadian Literature* (Toronto: House of Anansi Press, 1972), pp. 184–85.
6 Graeme Gibson, *Eleven Canadian Novelists* (Toronto: House of

Anansi Press, 1973), p. 21. Atwood is quoted as saying: "The marriage isn't real. She made it up."

7 Ibid., p. 22.
8 Atwood, *Survival.*
9 Ibid., p. 222.
10 Carol P. Christ, "Margaret Atwood: The Surfacing of Women's Spiritual Quest and Vision," *Signs: A Journal of Women in Culture and Society* 2, no. 2 (Winter 1976), p. 320.
11 Margaret Atwood, *The Journals of Susanna Moodie* (Toronto: Oxford University Press, 1970), p. 62.
12 Atwood, *Selected Poems*, p. 159.
13 Gibson, *Canadian Novelists*, p. 20.
14 Laing, *Divided Self*, p. 47.
15 Christ, "Margaret Atwood," p. 323.
16 Atwood, *Survival*, p. 63.
17 Ibid.
18 Christ, "Margaret Atwood," p. 325.
19 Atwood, *Survival*, p. 245.

THE SELF-CREATED OTHER

1 Jean Baker Miller, ed., *Psychoanalysis and Women* (Baltimore: Penguin Books, 1974).
2 Virginia Woolf, "Professions for Women," in *The Death of the Moth and Other Essays* (New York: Harcourt Brace, 1942), pp. 236–38.
3 Florence Howe and Ellen Bass, eds., *No More Masks! An Anthology of Poems by Women* (New York: Doubleday, 1973), p. 32.
4 Charlotte Perkins Gilman, *The Yellow Wallpaper* (Old Westbury, N.Y.: The Feminist Press, 1973).
5 Sylvia Plath, *The Bell Jar* (New York: Bantam Books, 1972), pp. 62–63. All subsequent references are to pages in this edition.
6 Sylvia Plath, *Ariel* (New York: Harper & Row, 1965), p. 50.
7 Elizabeth Hardwick, *Seduction and Betrayal: Women and Literature* (New York: Vintage, 1974), p. 111.

SELECTED
BIBLIOGRAPHY

Atwood, Margaret. *The Edible Woman*. New York: Little Brown, 1969.
———. *The Journals of Susanna Moodie*. Toronto: Oxford University Press, 1970.
———. *Selected Poems*. Toronto: Oxford University Press, 1976.
———. *Surfacing*. New York: Simon & Schuster, 1972.
———. *Survival: A Thematic Guide to Canadian Literature*. Toronto: House of Anansi Press, 1972.
Bachofen, J. J. *Myth, Religion, and Mother Right*. Princeton: Princeton University Press, 1954.
Bazin, Nancy Topping. *Virginia Woolf and the Androgynous Vision*. New Brunswick, N.J.: Rutgers University Press, 1973.
Beauvoir, Simone de. *The Second Sex*. New York: Alfred A. Knopf, 1953.
Beja, Morris. *Epiphany in the Modern Novel*. Seattle: University of Washington Press, 1971.
———. *Psychological Fiction*. Glenview, Ill.: Scott, Foresman, 1971.
Bell, Quentin. *Virginia Woolf: A Biography*. New York: Harcourt Brace Jovanovich, 1972.
Blackstone, Bernard. *Virginia Woolf: A Commentary*. London: Hogarth Press, 1949.
Boyers, Robert, ed. *R. D. Laing and Anti-Psychiatry*. New York: Harper & Row, 1971.
Brewster, Dorothy, *Doris Lessing*. New York: Twayne Publishers, 1965.
Brontë, Charlotte. *Jane Eyre*. Edited by June Jack and Margaret Smith. London: Oxford University Press, 1969.
———. *Villette*. New York: Harper & Row, 1972.
Brower, Reuben A. *The Fields of Light*. New York: Oxford University Press, 1968.

137

138   Selected Bibliography

Burkhart, Charles. *Charlotte Brontë: A Psychosexual Study of Her Novels.* London: Gollancz, 1973.

Burns, Wayne. "The Critical Relevance of Freudianism." *Western Review* 20 (1956), 301–14.

Chesler, Phyllis. *Women and Madness.* New York: Avon, 1972.

Christ, Carol P. "Margaret Atwood: The Surfacing of Women's Spiritual Quest and Vision." *Signs: A Journal of Women in Culture and Society* 2, no. 2 (Winter 1976), 316–30.

Craig, W. A. *The Brontë Novels.* London: Methuen, 1968.

Eagleton, Terry. *Myths of Power: A Marxist Study of the Brontës.* London: Macmillan, 1975.

Edel, Leon. *The Psychological Novel, 1900–1950.* New York: Lippincott, 1955.

Firestone, Shulamith. *The Dialectic of Sex: The Case for Feminist Revolution.* New York: William Morrow, 1970.

Fleishman, Aaron. *Virginia Woolf: A Critical Reading.* Baltimore: The Johns Hopkins University Press, 1975.

Fraiberg, Louis. *Psychoanalysis and American Literary Criticism.* Detroit: Wayne State University Press, 1960.

Friedan, Betty. *The Feminine Mystique.* New York: Norton, 1970.

Freud, Sigmund. *The New Complete Introductory Lectures on Psychoanalysis.* Edited and Translated by James Strachey. New York: Norton, 1966.

Gaskell, Elizabeth C. *The Life of Charlotte Brontë.* New York: Appleton, 1857.

Gelfant, Blanche. "Love and Conversion in *Mrs. Dalloway*." *Criticism* 8 (1966), 229–45.

Gerin, Winifred. *Charlotte Brontë: The Evolution of Genius.* London: Oxford University Press, 1967.

Gibson, Graeme. *Eleven Canadian Novelists.* Toronto: House of Anansi Press, 1973.

Gilman, Charlotte Perkins. *The Yellow Wallpaper.* Old Westbury, N.Y.: Feminist Press, 1973.

Gornick, Vivian, and Barbara K. Moran, eds. *Woman in Sexist Society: Studies in Power and Powerlessness.* New York: Mentor, 1971.

Greer, Germaine. *The Female Eunuch.* New York: Bantam, 1972.

Gregor, Ian, ed. *The Brontës: A Collection of Critical Essays.* Englewood Cliffs, N.J.: Prentice-Hall, 1970.

Harding, M. Esther. *Woman's Mysteries, Ancient and Modern.* New York: Bantam, 1973.

Hardwick, Elizabeth. *Seduction and Betrayal: Women and Literature.* New York: Vintage, 1974.

Selected Bibliography 139

Hawthorn, Jeremy. *Virginia Woolf's Mrs. Dalloway: A Study in Aliena-tion*. London: Sussex University Press, 1975.

Heilbrun, Carolyn. *Toward a Recognition of Androgyny*. New York: Alfred A. Knopf, 1973.

Heilman, R. A. "Charlotte Brontë: Reason and the Moon." *Nineteenth-Century Fiction* 14 (March 1960), 283–302.

Horney, Karen. *Feminine Psychology*. Edited by Harold Kelman. New York: Norton, 1967.

Howe, Florence. "Doris Lessing's Free Women." *The Nation* 11 (January 1965), 34–37.

Janeway, Elizabeth. *Man's World, Woman's Place: A Study in Social Mythology*. New York: Dell, 1971.

Kaplan, Janet Sydney. "The Limits of Consciousness in the Novels of Doris Lessing." *Contemporary Literature* 14 (1973), 541–44.

Keppler, C. F. *The Literature of the Second Self*. Tucson: University of Arizona Press, 1972.

Kiell, Norman, ed. *Psychoanalysis, Psychology, and Literature: A Bibliography*. Madison: University of Wisconsin Press, 1963.

Laing, R. D. *The Divided Self*. New York: Random House, 1969.

———. *The Politics of Experience*. New York, Random House, 1967.

———. *The Politics of the Family and Other Essays*. New York: Random House, 1969.

Laing, R. D. and A. Esterson. *Sanity, Madness and the Family*. New York: Basic Books, 1964.

Lessing, Doris. *The Four-Gated City*. New York: Alfred A. Knopf, 1969.

———. *The Golden Notebook*. New York: Simon & Schuster, 1962.

———. "To Room Nineteen." in *Women and Fiction*, edited by Susan Cahill. New York: New American Library, 1975.

Love, Jean O. *Worlds in Consciousness: Mythopoetic Thought in the Novels of Virginia Woolf*. Berkeley: University of California Press, 1970.

Marder, Herbert. *Feminism and Art*. Chicago: University of Chicago Press, 1968.

Martin, Robert B. *The Accents of Persuasion: Charlotte Brontë's Novels*. London: Faber & Faber, 1966.

Miller, Jean Baker, ed. *Psychoanalysis and Women*. Baltimore: Penguin, 1974.

Millett, Kate. *Sexual Politics*. New York: Doubleday, 1969.

Mitchell, Juliet. *Psychoanalysis and Feminism: Freud, Reich, Laing and Women*. New York: Random House, 1975.

———. *Woman's Estate*. New York: Random House, 1973.

Moglen, Helene. *Charlotte Brontë: The Self Conceived*. New York: Norton, 1976.

140   Selected Bibliography

Naremore, James. *The World Without a Self: Virginia Woolf and the Novel.* New Haven and London: Yale University Press, 1973.
O'Neill, Judith, ed. *Critics on Charlotte and Emily Brontë.* Coral Gables: University of Miami Press, 1968.
Peters, Margot. *Charlotte Brontë: Style in the Novel.* Madison: University of Wisconsin Press, 1973.
————. *Uniquiet Soul: A Biography of Charlotte Brontë.* New York: Doubleday, 1975.
Plath, Sylvia. *Ariel.* New York: Harper & Row, 1965.
————. *The Bell Jar.* New York: Bantam, 1972.
Rachman, Shalom. "Clarissa's Attic: Virginia Woolf's *Mrs. Dalloway* Reconsidered." *Twentieth-Century Literature* 18 (January 1972), 3–18.
Rank, Otto. *The Double: A Psychoanalytic Study.* Translated and edited by Harry Tucker, Jr. Chapel Hill: University of North Carolina Press, 1971.
Reich, Wilhelm. *Sex-Pol: Essays 1929–1934.* Edited by Lee Baxandall. New York: Vintage, 1972.
Rhys, Jean. *Wide Sargasso Sea.* New York: Norton, 1966.
Rich, Adrienne. "*Jane Eyre*: Temptations of a Motherless Woman." *MS.* 2, no. 4 (October 1973).
————. *Of Woman Born: Motherhood as Experience and Institution.* New York: Norton, 1976.
Richter, Harvena. *Virginia Woolf: The Inward Voyage.* Princeton: Princeton University Press, 1970.
Rogers, Robert. *A Psychoanalytic Study of the Double in Literature.* Detroit: Wayne State University Press, 1970.
Ruitenbeek, Hendrik M., ed. *Psychoanalysis and Literature.* New York: Dutton, 1964.
Schlueter, Paul. *The Novels of Doris Lessing.* Carbondale: Southern Illinois University Press, 1969.
Showalter, Elaine, ed. *Women's Liberation and Literature.* New York: Harcourt Brace Jovanovich, 1971.
Smith, David. "Incest Patterns in Two Victorian Novels," p. 1, "Her Master's Voice: *Jane Eyre* and the Incest Taboo." *Literature and Psychology* 15 (Summer 1965), 136–44.
Sprague, Claire, ed. *Virginia Woolf: A Collection of Critical Essays.* Englewood Cliffs, N.J.: Prentice Hall, 1971.
Strouse, Jean, ed. *Women and Analysis: Dialogues on Psychoanalytic Views of Femininity.* New York: Grosman, 1974.
Tymms, Ralph. *Doubles in Literary Psychology.* Cambridge: Bowes and Bowes, 1949.

Vicinus, Martha, ed. *Suffer and Be Still: Women in the Victorian Age.* Bloomington: Indiana University Press, 1973.

Vlastos, Marion. "Doris Lessing and R. D. Laing: Psychopolitics and Prophecy," *PMLA* 91, no. 2 (March 1976), 245–58.

Woolf, Leonard. *Beginning Again: An Autobiography of the Years 1911–1918.* London: Hogarth Press, 1964.

———. *Downhill All the Way: An Autobiography of the Years 1919–1939.* New York: Harcourt, Brace and World, 1967.

Woolf, Virginia. *Collected Essays.* New York: Harcourt, Brace and World, 1967.

———. *The Death of the Moth and Other Essays.* New York: Harcourt Brace, 1942.

———. *Mrs. Dalloway.* New York: Harcourt, Brace and World, 1925.

———. *A Room of One's Own.* New York: Harcourt, Brace and World, 1957.

———. *Three Guineas.* New York: Harcourt, Brace and World, 1938.

———. *To the Lighthouse.* New York: Harcourt, Brace and World, 1961.

———. *A Writer's Diary.* Edited by Leonard Woolf. New York: Harcourt, Brace, 1954.

Zwerdling, Alex. "*Mrs. Dalloway* and the Social System," *PMLA* 92, no. 1 (January 1977), 69–82.

INDEX

abortion, as symbolic of split self, in *Surfacing,* 96–97, 99, 100, 103, 106, 109, 110

Adele, in *Jane Eyre,* 24, 36

"Americans, the," in *Surfacing,* 11, 99, 100, 115

analyst-patient relationship. *See* therapeutic technique

androgyny: in *Jane Eyre,* 26; in *Mrs. Dalloway,* 42, 51, 54; in *Surfacing,* 93, 111

"Angel in the House, The," 120

Anna, in *Surfacing,* 94, 95, 102, 104, 105

apotheosis of psychotic personality, 12; in *Jane Eyre,* 27; in *Mrs. Dalloway,* 59, 62; in *The Four-Gated City,* 88; in *Surfacing,* 107–8, 111, 112–13

Ariel, 136*n6*

artist, role of, 56, 96, 102

Atwood, Margaret, 10, 12, 13, 91–115, 119, 120, 121, 122, 124, 125, 126, 127

Austen, Jane, 123

Bazin, Nancy Topping, 51

Beauvoir, Simone de, 4

Beja, Morris, 55, 58

Bell Jar, The, 124–26

Bessie, in *Jane Eyre,* 34

bigamy, in *Jane Eyre,* 19, 24

bildungsroman, 74

Bradshaw, Sir William, in *Mrs. Dalloway,* 11, 50, 60, 61, 62; as personification of social system, 44; compared to St. John Rivers and Rev. Brocklehurst, 45; relation to Lady Bradshaw, 47–48; compared to Dr. Lamb, 80–81

Brewster, Dorothy, 69–70

Briefing for a Descent into Hell, 88

Briscoe, Lily, in *To the Lighthouse,* 52

Brocklehurst, Reverend, in *Jane Eyre,* 11, 17, 18, 20, 22; compared to Sir William Bradshaw, 45

Brontë, Charlotte, 10, 12, 15–37, 41, 42, 43, 49, 61, 62, 68, 69, 70, 72, 73, 77, 79, 94, 100, 119, 120, 121, 122, 124, 126, 127

Brontë Novels, The, 132*n2*

"Brontës: A Centennial Observance, The," 132*n4*

Burns, Helen, in *Jane Eyre,* 19, 20, 30, 34

"bushing," as theme in *Surfacing,* 114

Byronic hero, in *Jane Eyre,* 19, 23

cameras, images of, in *Surfacing,* 94–95, 103, 107

Caroline, in *The Four-Gated City,* 87

castration, symbolic, in *Jane Eyre,* 16, 26, 31, 32

castration complex, female, 4

chains, images of, in *Jane Eyre,* 21–22, 25, 31

Charlotte Brontë: Style in the Novel, 19–20, 33, 36

Charlotte Brontë: The Evolution of Genius, 132*n9*

Charlotte Brontë: The Self Conceived, 16, 18, 23, 26, 32, 37

Chase, Richard, 132*n4*

chastity, as value: in *Jane Eyre,* 33; in *Mrs. Dalloway,* 49, 50

Chesler, Phyllis, 3, 4–5, 6, 12

childhood, images of, 85–86, 88, 98–99

Children of Violence, 68

Christ, Carol P., 98, 107, 110, 115

Cocteau, Jean, 56

Coldridge, Lynda, in *The Four-Gated City,* 106, 123; as guide and doppelgänger, 77–78; compared to

Index

"Margaret Atwood: The Surfacing
of Women's Spiritual Quest and
Vision," 98, 110, 115
Marian, in *The Edible Woman*, 97, 101
marriage, images of, 121; in *Jane
Eyre*, 31–32; in *Mrs. Dalloway*, 47,
48, 49, 50–51; in *The Four-Gated
City*, 71–72; in *Surfacing*, 96, 103,
105
Mason, Bertha, in *Jane Eyre*, 15, 17,
18, 20, 22, 62, 123; as Jane's double, 16, 26, 28; her capacity for
passion, 23; compared to Jane, 24;
loss of sexual identity, 24, 26; as
androgynous, 26; as scapegoat, 27;
as subject for *Wide Sargasso Sea*, 27;
as agent of Rochester's fall, 27, 31;
compared with Septimus Warren
Smith, 61; compared with Lynda
Coldridge, 77–80; as witch, 83; as
mirror image, 94
mental hospitals. *See* confinement as
punishment; therapeutic technique
Miller, Jean Baker, 4, 5, 7, 119
Millett, Kate, 4, 6, 29–30
mirror, images of, 10, 122; in *Jane
Eyre*, 18, 28; in *The Four-Gated City*,
77; in *Surfacing*, 94–95, 113
Mitchell, Juliet, 5–6, 8
Moglen, Helene, 16–17, 18, 23–24,
26, 32, 37
moon, images of, in *Jane Eyre*, 35; in
Surfacing, 99, 103, 108, 109, 110,
113
Morgan, Robin, 65
mother, the search for, 11–12; in
Jane Eyre, 35–36; in *Mrs. Dalloway*,
51–52; in *The Four-Gated City*, 79,
86; in *Surfacing*, 110; as aligned
with nature, 111—13; as guide toward self integration, 122—23
motherhood, attitudes toward: in
Jane Eyre, 36, 37; in *The Four-Gated
City*, 86–87; in *Surfacing*, 110, 112,
115
Moulton, Ruth, 4

Mrs. Dalloway, 4, 8, 11, 41–63, 67, 75,
76, 121, 123, 125
"*Mrs. Dalloway* and the Social Sys-
tem," 43–44
*Myths of Power: A Marxist Study of the
Brontës*, 26

name, loss of and loss of identity,
121; in *Jane Eyre*, 21; in *Mrs. Dalloway*, 49; in *The Four-Gated City*,
76; in *Surfacing*, 93; in *The Bell Jar*,
125
Naremore, James, 58
nature, woman identified with, 99,
100, 101, 104, 111–13
*No More Masks! An Anthology of Poems
by Women*, 136n3
nuclear family, and oppression of
women, 9
Nussey, Ellen, 22, 31

*Of Woman Born: Motherhood as Experi-
ence and Institution*, 11, 34, 137n30
"On Being Ill," 48–49
ontological insecurity, 115, 121; in
Jane Eyre, 20–21, 25; in *Mrs. Dalloway*, 41, 53

palmistry, 95–96, 110
passion, as kind of insanity in *Jane
Eyre*, 32–33
"Patient and Patriarch: Women in
the Psycho-therapeutic Relationship," 4–5
Peters, Margot, 19–20, 30–31, 33, 36,
133n14
pill, the, 103–4
Plath, Sylvia, 123, 124–26
Poe, Edgar Allen, 122
Politics of Experience, The, 9, 42, 47,
55, 56, 60, 69, 86, 132nn19,
24,25,5, 134nn30,31,32,33,
135nn5,6,9,12,13,15,16,18,19
Politics of the Family, The, 132n21
Poole, Grace, in *Jane Eyre*, 26, 27
pregnancy, images of, in *Jane Eyre*,
36

126; in *Jane Eyre*, 16; in *Mrs. Dalloway*, 42–46, 52; in *The Four-Gated City*, 67–70; in *Surfacing*, 100, 112, 114, 115
"sound-barrier, the," in *The Four-Gated City*, 84
subjectivity as theme in Lessing's works, 70, 71–74
suicide, psychological or physical, 21, 25, 31, 44, 48, 60, 61–62, 73, 94, 123, 125
supernatural, references to: in *Jane Eyre*, 24, 35; in *The Four-Gated City*, 83–84; in *Surfacing*, 111–12
Surfacing, 5, 91–115, 120, 121, 123, 125
Survival: A Thematic Guide to Canadian Literature, 96, 98, 111, 114, 115
Symonds, Alexandra, 4

Temple, Miss, in *Jane Eyre*, 34
therapeutic technique, opposition to traditional forms of in analyst-patient relationships, 10; shock therapy, 80; drug therapy, 81; analyst as authority, 81–82; mental hospitals, 82, 86
Thompson, Clara, 4
Thornfield Hall, in *Jane Eyre*, 15, 18, 28, 35
Three Guineas, 9, 43
time, significance of, in *Mrs. Dalloway*, 41, 51, 57, 59
To Bedlam and Part Way Back, 117
"To Room Nineteen," 72, 73
To the Lighthouse, 48, 49, 52, 54, 61
Toward a Recognition of Androgyny, 32
trees, images of, in *Mrs. Dalloway*, 41, 51, 57, 59

Unquiet Soul: A Biography of Charlotte Brontë, 133nn14,26

vaginal orgasm, theory of, 4

Victorian standards for womanhood, 23, 26, 30, 31, 33, 120, 123
Villette, 29–30, 37
"Virginia Woolf," by E. M. Forster, 133n5, 134n34
Virginia Woolf: A Critical Reading, 60
Virginia Woolf: The Inward Voyage, 61
Virginia Woolf and the Androgynous Vision, 51
Virginia Woolf's Mrs. Dalloway: A Study in Alienation, 52
virility, as negative attribute in *Mrs. Dalloway*, 43, 45
vision, symbolic references to, 68, 94, 95, 103
"Visit to Toronto, with Companions, A," 13
Vlastos, Marion, 80, 135n2

Walsh, Peter, in *Mrs. Dalloway*, 48, 61
war: in *Mrs. Dalloway*, 43; in *The Four-Gated City*, 68, 69, 71; in *Surfacing*, 98–99
Weisstein, Naomi, 5, 6
Wide Sargasso Sea, 27–28
witches, references to, 83, 111–12
Woman's Estate, 5–6
Woman's Mysteries, 35
Women and Madness, 3, 4, 131n14, 132n27
Woolf, Virginia, 4, 8, 9, 10, 12, 22, 41–63, 69, 70, 72, 73, 75, 77, 80, 82–83, 93, 100, 104, 111, 119–20, 121, 124, 125, 126, 127
Worlds in Consciousness: Mythopoetic Thought in the Novels of Virginia Woolf, 58
World Without a Self, The: Virginia Woolf and the Novel, 58
Writer's Diary, A, 133n1, 134nn8,23

Yellow Wallpaper, The, 79, 123–24

Zwerdling, Alex, 43–44